Scripture Discussion Con

SCRIPTURE DISCUSSION COMMENTARY 9

Series editor: Laurence Bright

John

John   *Giles Hibbert*
1 John   *Bernard Robinson*
James   *Laurence Bright*

ACTA Foundation
Adult Catechetical Teaching Aids
Chicago, Illinois

First published 1972
ACTA Foundation (Adult Catechetical Teaching Aids),
4848 N. Clark Street, Chicago, Illinois 60640

Nihil obstat : John M. T. Barton STD LSS   *Censor*
Imprimatur : + Victor Guazzelli   *Vicar General*
Westminster, 3 July 1972

Library of Congress number 71–173033
ISBN 0 87946 008 3
Made and printed in Great Britain by
William Clowes & Sons, Limited
London, Beccles and Colchester

Contents

Contents

Contents

vii

General Introduction

A few of the individual units which make up this series of biblical commentaries have already proved their worth issued as separate booklets. Together with many others they are now grouped together in a set of twelve volumes covering almost all the books of the old and new testaments—a few have been omitted as unsuitable to the general purpose of the series.

That purpose is primarily to promote discussion. This is how these commentaries differ from the others that exist. They do not cover all that could be said about the biblical texts, but concentrate on the features most likely to get lively conversation going—those, for instance, with special relevance for later developments of thought, or for life in the church and world of today. For this reason passages of narrative are punctuated by sets of questions designed to get a group talking, though the text of scripture, helped by the remarks of the commentator, should have already done just that.

For the text is what matters. Individuals getting ready for a meeting, the group itself as it meets, should always have the bible centrally present, and use the commentary only as a tool. The bibliographies will help those wishing to dig deeper.

What kinds of group can expect to work in this way?

Absolutely any. The bible has the reputation of being difficult, and in some respects it is, but practice quickly clears up a lot of initial obstacles. So parish groups of any kind can and should be working on it. The groups needn't necessarily already exist, it is enough to have a few like-minded friends and to care sufficiently about finding out what the bible means. Nor need they be very large; one family could be quite enough. High schools (particularly in the senior year), colleges and universities are also obvious places for groups to form. If possible they should everywhere be ecumenical in composition: though all the authors are Roman catholics, there is nothing sectarian in their approach.

In each volume there are two to four or occasionally more studies of related biblical books. Each one is self-contained; it is neither necessary nor desirable to start at the beginning and plough steadily through. Take up, each time, what most interests you—there is very little in scripture that is actually dull! Since the commentaries are by different authors, you will discover differences of outlook, in itself a matter for discussion. Above all, remember that getting the right general approach to reading the bible is more important than answering any particular question about the text—and that this approach only comes with practice.

Volume 9 contains the last and most profound of the gospels, that of John, together with the first of the letters associated with it (the other two are too short to be of much interest). The letter of James, probably written much earlier, is also included.

L. B.

John

Giles Hibbert

Introduction

Fact, fiction, and theology

At first sight the fourth gospel looks widely different from the other three; its style and tone, together with what it is setting out to do, appear to be of a different order. Whereas the synoptic gospels seem to be more or less historical accounts of the life and ministry of Jesus of Nazareth, the fourth gospel appears to be high theological speculation on that theme, not altogether accurately welded to the same set of facts. The opening words of Luke's gospel show us the difference in approaches: Matthew starts by tying in the gospel with the past history of Israel, Mark with the preaching of John the Baptist; in contrast John's begins with the word of God in the timeless presence of God, using language which constitutes one of the finest passages of poetry in the bible.

Fortunately our understanding of the synoptic gospels at least has progressed to the point at which we no longer take such a simple and naive view of them. It is now realised to what extent the authors, even (perhaps especially) in the case of the shortest and apparently simplest gospel, that of Mark, have theological visions to present and are in no straightforward way presenting us with a 'life of Christ'; they are offering us a theological and dramatic

3

presentation of the way in which God's gift to men—his salvation—is brought about and made a reality amongst us. Is the fourth gospel in any way fundamentally different?

There is a sense in which it is no different, its manner of presentation of 'the good news' is similarly theological and dramatic rather than biographical; nevertheless it also differs considerably in style and outlook from the other gospels—it represents a separate tradition with its distinctive outlook. Thus it is only when it has become possible to see the structure and content of the fourth gospel in the light of its author's context, style of thinking and overall intention, that one can throw off the urge to make the wrong sort of comparisons with the style of the synoptics and thus free oneself from the dangers of seriously misunderstanding John.

Once one has made these provisos one can safely give one's attention to the fact that the fourth gospel is indeed distinctively theological in an intensive way; one can note that the whole 'school of life', and reflection upon it, from which it arose would seem to have been engaged in exploring the meaning of Christ's work amongst us in a way not witnessed to in the other gospels. But if the theology is high-flying—giving rise to the eagle as the gospel's symbol—it is nevertheless something firmly located within reality; and the poetic expression, together with dramatic structure, which the gospel so often employs to achieve its effect may well provide us with a more powerful, and even more authentic, presentation of the way in which God is actually present to men in the person of Jesus of Nazareth than would be achieved by any mere recitation of the details of his ministry, or even perhaps than any catalogue of his actual sayings.

These are the two points which we need to keep our eyes upon throughout the reading of this gospel. Apart from helping us to understand its message, it may also help us to see how theology on the one hand, and poetic and dramatic form on the other, can in fact join together to constitute a true engagement with, rather than anything like a flight from, the reality of a world in which God has manifested himself in intimate communion with men. But they will only achieve this in as far as they are rooted in the actual historical circumstances of the man in whom that communion achieved its perfection—Jesus of Nazareth. To see this in action is surely one of the primary reasons for studying this gospel.

Origins and history

(i) The tradition

The question of the origination of the fourth gospel— where it was written, by whom, and for what sort of an audience—indeed the whole question of the context from which it emerges and in which it was formed, takes on a greater importance in this case than in that of the other gospels. In their case it does not add all that much to one's understanding of what is written in them; it matters relatively little who actually wrote them. In the case of Luke the connection with Paul is internally indicated, and its differences in outlook from his are equally clear. In our understanding of the development of the early church, that Mark's gospel embodies the basic teaching of Peter is important, but it only adds a little to our appreciation of what he is saying. Matthew equally speaks for itself, though the whole question of its Aramaic origin, and the way in which it came to be translated and re-written in Greek, is of considerable importance in appreciating it deeply.

With John, however, the question of authorship, and particularly of context, is far more important. Because it seems, in its poetical, dramatic and theological presentation, to be further removed from historical actuality than do the synoptics, the questions of origination become all the more significant. Some appreciation of when, and by what group of people the gospel was written, enables one to approach it without danger of misrepresentation.

The authorship of the gospel of John is complex. On whatever basis one approaches it is clear that there are considerable discontinuities and even what seem to be abrupt changes of direction in the train of thought. These have to be accounted for if one is to appreciate the work's overall communication—or in other words the gospel.

Several theories have been put forward to account for these inconsistencies in the text as it has come down to us, varying from the simple suggestion that it is a relatively haphazard compilation of early christian (or gnostic) texts all bearing in a more or less similar way on the same subject, to the suggestion that the original sheets on which it was written got jumbled up at some stage and thus passages of the same length need re-arranging to produce the coherent original! Such a theory as this latter demands too many improbable coincidences to be acceptable however ingeniously it may have been argued (as for example by F. R. Hoare in *The Original Order and Chapters of St John's Gospel*); the other alternative, though a little nearer the truth, seems exaggerated, and also makes too many suppositions.

There are also those, however, who argue, from a respectable critical position, that the gospel as it stands is in fact a whole and makes sense as a whole. It is in actual fact not too difficult to reconcile both this position and the recognition that there are discontinuities due to different hands at work in the authorship; and this can be done without having to impose theories derived outside of tradition or the internal evidence of the work itself. The niceties of the arguments involved need not be considered here; they are to be found in the appropriate works (see bibliography); what is to be presented is the theory of authorship which seems best explained by the text of the gospel as it stands and by what can be gathered of the milieu from which it emerged, and it is hoped that this will provide the necessary framework for interpreting its contents.

The composition of the fourth gospel would seem to consist of five stages. First of all there is the existence and transmission, largely within an early christian community, of traditional material concerning the sayings and actions of Jesus—not dissimilar to the material which makes up the synoptic tradition, but which is independent of it.

The second stage consists of the development of this material over probably several decades in a particular way which is characteristic of the style and concerns of this gospel. This is a period of teaching and preaching, and of theological speculation forced by the circumstances of a living rather than static situation; and it is the period of the critical formulation of the gospel as the thing which we know. This is when the miracles and sayings of Jesus would have been appraised and seen in their overall context, and when the great dramatic dialogues focusing around particular incidents would have been built up. What is characteristic of such material is that on the one hand it belongs to a living situation of pastoral activity and on the other that it is dominated by the thought of a single person or of a school of like-minded men working closely together. At this stage, however, nothing would have been definitely (if at all) written down.

The third stage is that in which the gospel first appears as a distinct written work—in other words the first edition of the fourth gospel. Two points should be noted here. First of all it is more than likely that the dominant figure of the school within which the development has taken place should be either directly or indirectly the author of this edition. If it were written after his death (though there is internal evidence, to be mentioned below, which makes this unlikely) it would equally likely to have been written on his behalf and in his name. Thus in a sense, whether directly or indirectly, the main tradition bearer, or in other words the man whose mind is so clearly at the centre of this work, can be called the author of this gospel—whether his name be John or not. The second point to note is that the actual compilation of a 'gospel' from the material being handed on and developed in the preceding stage would necessarily be selective. There could easily be material still alive in the tradition which was not incorporated in this first edition.

The fourth stage consists of a single or a series of revisions of the text by the same hand who wrote it, which can be seen to have been prompted by the need for different emphases as the result of historical circumstances, such for example as the excommunication from the synagogue of Jews who continued to believe in Jesus. To explain the actual text of the gospel it is not necessary in fact to posit more than one actual such revision, though it also has to be admitted that it is far from possible to distinguish with any exactitude later revisions by the same hand from the original text.

The fifth and final stage is another revision, or rather

redaction, but this time clearly by another hand; though at the same time this editor would seem to have been closely related to the evangelist himself—probably a personal friend or disciple. (For a further note on this relationship, see below under the heading of authorship.) He is clearly within the same tradition which has gone to make the earlier stages; and he is also in possession of a considerable quantity of other 'Johannine' material, sometimes slight variants on what is already in the original. He adds to this latter without revising (treating it with apparently great respect), and it is these additions which cause the breaks in continuity in the gospel which are so obvious. They are, however, far from being arbitrary, the way in which they are incorporated indicating a similar theological mind and a clear understanding of the original. From the ending of the gospel it would seem clear that this final redaction took place upon the death of a person of considerable importance in the church, in all probability the evangelist himself, and maybe—critical opinion is once more swinging round to this possibility—this is actually John the Apostle (see below).

This leads us to the question of the identity of the figure central to the Johannine tradition; in other words it is now the nature of *stage one* that we want to look at. The fourth gospel appears on the surface to be an 'historical account' of the acts of Jesus, as do the synoptic gospels. Despite the fact that it seems to be built up out of a body of *kerygma* (primitive preaching) in the same way that the synoptics are, it presents so many differences from them and even contradictions that people have queried whether it has any actual historical value at all with regard to the life and ministry of Christ. It has been suggested that it was written simply to preserve the

christian theological tradition from becoming too mythological, too spiritualistic, by tying down its speculation
to an actual 'life of Jesus'. Indeed this is a worthy motive,
but if it lacks basis in fact its value is very considerably
diminished. So the question before us is whether the
fourth gospel represents an imitation of the 'historical
gospel' style, or whether it in fact represents a primitive
tradition, equal in status to, and distinct from, that
behind the synoptics, together with its subsequent
development.

Recent archaeological exploration in Palestine has
shown that many of the particular details concerning
Jerusalem and the country around it, which are peculiar
to the fourth gospel, are in fact correct in detail and must
have come from someone who knew it before its destruction by the Romans. But more importantly the discovery
of the Qumran scrolls has indicated that patterns of
thought occurring in John, which had been regarded as
much later and as coming from sources outside judaism,
were in fact very much in existence at the time of Christ;
and they also show a living link between the thought of
John's gospel and that of the old testament. For this
reason so many of the theories about the gospel which
antedate the Qumran discoveries, especially those
emphasising the Greek nature of its thought, must be
dismissed as being built around disproven hypotheses. It
should be noted too that these hypotheses have been
based upon pure supposition rather than actual tradition
or the text of the gospel, which alone can give objective
critical assessment.

It is interesting to note that where the material in
John's gospel differs in detail from that in the synoptics
there does not seem to be any indication of deliberate
changes, or even of misunderstandings of a supposed

original. One either has to suppose the existence of a separate tradition or that the author of the fourth gospel just arbitrarily and whimsically changed the details as he went along incorporating the synoptic tradition into his work—a procedure which would not help its acceptance by the early church as an authentic gospel. Also it is interesting to note that whereas the agreements between John and the synoptics are considerable there does not appear to be any especial agreement with any one of them over against the others—a feature equally pointing to a separate tradition. There are of course a few incidents of direct borrowings from the synoptic tradition. Some scholars have noted a particular relation in places to the emergent Lucan gospel tradition. It is also difficult to say whether there are any cross-influences present in the material added by the final redactor (*stage five*).

All in all the evidence of the actual text suggests that the fourth gospel is based upon a tradition linking it with the life of Jesus as authentic, and in part as primitive, as that which goes to constitute the synoptic gospels. Nevertheless it would be folly to attempt a reconstruction of the chronological details of Jesus' life and ministry on the basis of this gospel—it is not in any way meant to be that sort of presentation of him, and contains far too much arrangement of its material. At the same time, however, it may well be that with regard to some points, as for example the extent of the actual ministry of Jesus, the number of times that he went up to Jerusalem, and also some of the details of his arrest and passion, it is John's account rather than that of the synoptics which is 'historically' accurate.

(ii) The authorship

The question which now has to be asked is why, where,

when and by whom the fourth gospel was written, taking into account what has so far been said. First of all one should say that if the gospel is the product of historical tradition and authentic theological development the most likely motive for its being written is simply the preservation of these features. Nevertheless there will inevitably be extraneous factors which govern the actual form which such preservation takes, and thus it is not unreasonable to ask why, and for whom, the work was written—both originally and in its later editions.

Some people have suggested that the whole gospel was written as a tract against the sectarians of John the Baptist, but this theory, in any simple form, does not have much to support it; it is almost entirely hypothetical and the gospel contains as much material honouring John as it does placing him in true perspective with regard to Jesus. Others have wanted to see the fourth gospel as a work directed specifically against the early christian heretics, especially the docetists; but whereas this is obviously true in a vague and indefinite sense it is stretching the text far too far to see in it any specifically anti-heretical intention.

What is much clearer is that this gospel is in a very particular way concerned with judaism and with a Jewish (though not Palestinian) audience. It is in fact at the same time both very Jewish and in a sense extremely anti-Jewish. It, more than any other gospel, condemns 'the Jews' and shows how Jesus fulfils the apocalyptic expectation of the old testament and replaces its characteristic and specific institutions. This particular concern with the Jews has a twofold aspect: firstly there is the condemnation of those official representatives of judaism who rejected Jesus' claims (and those of his disciples) and persecuted him and his followers; secondly the gospel is

particularly concerned with addressing itself to those
Jewish christians who were still within the synagogue
and, after the destruction of Jerusalem and the temple,
were more and more being persecuted by those Jews who
totally rejected Christ.

The characteristic antagonism to 'the Jews' of the
fourth gospel has itself a twofold aspect. On the one hand
it represents the conflict between Jesus and the representatives of national authority in a clearly black and
white manner in order to bring out the nature of the
way in which the law was fulfilled by Jesus and his
approach to and acceptance of men rather than by the
narrow legalism and backward-looking rigidity of the
authorities. On the other hand it expresses a reaction to
the even narrower rejection of christian claims by the
Jewish religious leaders after the fall of Jerusalem—as
already mentioned. Herein lies the explanation of an
interesting anachronism which has affected important
terminology in this gospel.

This is the use of the term 'the Jews' to describe the
opponents of Jesus. We learn from the other gospels that
these were the scribes and pharisees above all others; in
John these same people are simply 'the Jews'. It has been
suggested that the term is antisemitic and represents the
reaction of a hellenistic christian group eager to gain
ascendency for its interpretation of christianity. This in
turn has been used to bolster the theory that the thought
of the fourth gospel is essentially Greek rather than
Hebraic. But these theories are entirely gratuitous, and
the reality is in fact both simpler and less contrived—we
have already noted how the Qumran discoveries have
put paid to the suggestion that the thought of the fourth
gospel is un-Hebraic. The term 'the Jews' is to be taken
in the sense that the word would have had at the time the

gospel must have been written. After the fall of Jerusalem and the final dispersion of the Jewish people it was precisely the pharisees who rallied the remnants and inaugurated the rigid doctrinal discipline which was to ensure its continuance. Judaism after this period, especially after the council of Jamnia (in the last decades of the century), was precisely pharisaic; 'the Jews' were the people who now more rigorously than ever were rejecting the claims of christians and attempting to purify judaism from this taint, and they were in direct continuation with those who originally opposed Jesus—thus for 'John' and his circle of christians 'the Jews' and 'the pharisees' were terms effectively synonymous.

There is nothing at all anti-semitic in John. Indeed the term 'Jews' or 'Jewish' is used frequently in the gospel in an entirely neutral sense. John does not reject judaism but those who have now become its exclusive official representatives. It is the christians—whether they be Jew or gentile—who are now to be seen as the true Israelites. It is interesting to note that whereas the synoptics condemn the pharisees as hypocrites and oppressors of the people, John precisely condemns them because they reject Jesus and are thus no longer the true heirs of Israel, or in other words the people of God; they belong to darkness outside the kingdom of God.

This is the nature of John's thinking, and the actual gospel is the expression of its implications and content. That brings us to a final point which is not unimportant. This is to stress that although the fourth gospel may thus have a particular Jewish and also anti-Jewish (in the above sense) slant, nevertheless it must be seen as being primarily an expression, addressed to believers, of the implications and context of their faith.

After what has now been said it can be seen that

accurate knowledge of exactly where, when and by whom this gospel was written is no longer going to be of acute importance to our understanding of it. Nevertheless what can be determined with regard to this, especially in the matter of dating, is going to help knit together our picture of its emergence, and thus its message, into a whole.

It used to be argued that because of the great theological development to be found in John it must be considerably later than the synoptics. We have seen already how this is partly refuted by the discoveries at Qumran, but it is also demonstrably an invalid argument since much Pauline material, now recognised as being earlier than the synoptics, is equally developed theologically. This is not something which took ages to appear, it began to happen the moment that living christian communities became a reality.

It used also to be thought that there was no evidence of John's gospel being known by the church at large until the end of the second century; it has now however been shown that Ignatius of Antioch must have known the gospel in the earliest years of the century, and Clement of Rome some fifteen years earlier exhibits knowledge of a similar theological thought and vocabulary. At the other end of the scale, for reasons already given, it would seem that the gospel, in its final edition at any rate, cannot have been written before or much before the council of Jamnia. Its probable date is between 90–100 AD, though the outside limits would have to be regarded as being 75–110 AD. Since the historical tradition underlying the formation of the gospel seems to go back, as something distinct in its own right and independent of the synoptic tradition, to something like 40–60 AD, this leaves a period of something like forty years for its development, initial writing and final editing—a situation conforming very well with the material as we have it.

Ephesus is the place traditionally associated with the writing of this gospel, and the conditions there would fit in very well with what we have seen. There are also considerable interrelationships between John and Revelation, both with regard to theological outlook and underlying tradition, and the latter book is clearly associated with Ephesus. It is interesting to note also that of all the Pauline literature Colossians and Ephesians have, like John, associations with the thought of Qumran. The evidence is not conclusive but it is certainly persuasive that our gospel originally emerged from a thriving christian community in precisely this area of Asia Minor in the final years of the first century.

Tradition has made the author of the fourth gospel John the son of Zebedee, one of the twelve. But it has to be acknowledged that tradition—even the earliest strands of it in this case—is considerably muddled on the point. The trouble is that there were far too many Johns around at that time, all of whom have claims of one sort or another to the authorship. We have mention of 'John the disciple of the Lord' who may or may not be John the son of Zebedee; there is John Mark, the companion of Barnabas and Paul; there is John the Presbyter, who may be one of these others or who may be distinct. And then there is 'the beloved disciple' of the gospel, who may or may not have to be identified with John the son of Zebedee.

There has in modern times been a tendency to favour John the Presbyter, mentioned by Papias, as author of the gospel. This may well be the man mentioned later as being a bishop of Ephesus, apparently appointed there by

John the Apostle. The trouble with this theory is that
there is as much evidence against it as for it—in fact the
same evidence can be used either way. Theories sup-
porting John Mark as author fare no better, but at the
same time the theory that the author is John the Apostle
is plagued with similar difficulties.

In this situation it is only possible to look within the
gospel itself to see what evidence it has to give. But here
the picture is no clearer, it is even in some senses more
complicated; nevertheless overall a pattern does emerge
which at any rate favours, if it does not prove, one particular solution. The gospel itself claims eye-witness
account for its authority (cf 19:26–27 and 21:24) and
this witness is identified mysteriously as 'the disciple
whom Jesus loved'. There are several candidates for the
role: Lazarus, John Mark, some otherwise unmentioned
disciple, and of course John, the son of Zebedee. There
is also the suggestion that 'the disciple whom Jesus
loves' is figurative for the exemplary christian or the
hellenistic church over against unbelieving judaism.

The suggestion that Lazarus is the beloved disciple
does solve one or two minor problems (though the theory
that the name is a pseudonym for John is altogether too
far-fetched.) His being John Mark solves several more,
particularly the problems connected with his entry into
the high priests' house at Jesus' 'trial', as similarly do
other theories suggesting that he was an unnamed
disciple who lived in Jerusalem. Nevertheless they introduce even greater problems. Once one has realised that
John's gospel is not simply late christian theologising, or
alternatively alien (eg hellenistic) thought being tacked
on to the life and message of Jesus, and has realised that
underlying it there is a tradition as venerable and
authentic as that behind the synoptics, one has got to give

just consideration, at least, to the 'eye-witness' accounts referred to in the fourth gospel in connection with 'the beloved disciple'. And the only reasons for believing that these accounts remain fictitious are the result of the unattested hypothesis that the source of the tradition behind John is not one of the twelve. Once one has accepted the possibility of an authentic tradition and of an eye-witness behind, or at the basis of, the theology of John, internal evidence, in relation to the evidence of the synoptics, suggests (though certainly cannot be said to prove) that the witness is in fact John, the son of Zebedee. A further point that should be added is that when one considers how oddly different, in many ways, this tradition is in detail from the synoptics, it is difficult to see how the gospel would have gained its initial acceptance if it only rested on the evidence of someone whom the synoptic gospels do not even mention as being in Jesus' inner circle. The actual anonymity of the witness (whatever we think of this) argues clean against the suggestion that the gospel has been edited precisely to make its acceptance by the church all the easier.

There remain two major difficulties with regard to the 'John' of the gospel being John the son of Zebedee. First of all there is the problem of access to the high priest's house during the trial. That John was purveyor of fish to the priestly high table (it would have been pretty high by the time it arrived from Galilee) is a ridiculously far-fetched idea; there is, however, internal evidence of a different kind in connection with this that has some plausibility. Comparison of the individual synoptics', together with John's, account of those present at the foot of the cross indicate that John was quite possibly a cousin of Jesus' through their respective mothers (see R. Brown, *The Gospel according to John*). Furthermore, if the infancy narratives in Luke, at least in their less typological aspects, have any narrow historical validity—and they seem to emerge from a primitive tradition centred on Jerusalem—we learn from them that Mary was in fact related to the priestly house. In the light of this John's access ceases to appear so unlikely. One might also add that the considerable emphasis given by the fourth gospel to Jerusalem, which would be strange coming from a Galilean disciple, becomes more understandable if the disciples went up to Jerusalem with Jesus not once, but on a number of occasions, as there is now evidence for believing. Nevertheless the primary reason for this emphasis is clearly theological.

The second difficulty concerns the style of the gospel, which is not something one would expect from a Galilean fisherman. It is not, however, being suggested that John the Apostle actually wrote it, but rather that he is at the centre of the tradition in which it was formed. It is interesting to note that in the parts representing the earlier editions the eye-witness referred to is consistently described as 'the other disciple' whereas it is in the final redaction that this character is described as and identified as 'the disciple whom Jesus loved'. It is easy to envisage the actual author as having a similar relationship to John as the latter did to Jesus, and under these conditions the whole literary usage becomes not perplexing but understandable.

Theological perspectives

One of the most notable of the theological aspects of the fourth gospel is its rigorous dualism. There is a radical division between light and darkness, truth and falsehood. Men belong to two camps: those who receive the word, and those who reject it. There is nothing half way in John; everything is black or white. 'I know your works: you are neither cold nor hot. Would that you were cold or hot! So, because you are lukewarm, and neither cold nor hot, I will spew you out of my mouth' (Rev 3:15). This epitomises, in its crudest form, an outlook running through and through the Johannine writings.

What is of the utmost importance is to understand the nature of this dualism. Is it ontological, intellectual, mystical, political or revolutionary? How does it affect one's whole way of looking at the world, at oneself, and at one's fellow man? How does it show one the full implications of one's accepting Christ, and what exactly is it asking one to accept? Does it represent the actual thought and outlook of Jesus himself, or is it a distortion arising entirely out of remoteness, both in time and context, from the figure portrayed?

These are questions for the gospel itself to answer. Some of them have, however, been touched on in part in the consideration already given to the origins of the gospel, and there are still aspects which need further preliminary clarification. What requires attention is the part played in the gospel by different strands of intellectual influence—Jewish, hellenistic and oriental.

It has been argued that one of the major influences on John came from an early form of gnosticism. Gnosticism in general has, as one of its primary characteristics, a dualism which, superficially at any rate, resembles that of the fourth gospel. It also has a prominent role for a saviour figure to lead men from the darkness into light. Recognising that by and large gnosticism has been a christian heresy rather than anything else, Bultmann for example posited an early pre-christian form which he associated with baptist sects in Palestine together with

the later mandaean sect in Mesopotamia. His reconstruction (cf his *Primitive Christianity*) is based first on what
he presumed to be non-christian in John and secondly
on what he imagined a baptising sect in Palestine at the
time of Christ to be like. The former represents a clear
case of *petitio principii*, and the latter has been discredited
by what we now know of such a sect at Qumran. In fact
the theory entirely lacks evidence. There are indeed
similarities between John and later (authentic) gnosticism, but it would seem that this is due to a common source
(judaic and christian) rather than to any dependence of
the former on the latter.

The theory that John's gospel is essentially hellenistic
has fared equally badly. Of course it is recognised that
there was already an important influence from Greek
thought present in judaism at the time of Christ; its
impact is to be found in the development of the wisdom
literature. But what is being questioned here is whether
there was in fact any influence of Greek thought, coming
to John from outside, such as to make him reinterpret the
gospel in hellenistic terms. Some of the most attractive
writers on the fourth gospel have assumed this position.

Most of the apparent parallels between John's thought
and that of platonism are in fact artificial and depend
upon the nature of the 'dualism' involved not being fully
appreciated. For example platonist dualism has to do
with the reality of the mind and thought over against the
material world, whereas Hebraic dualism is radically
religious and is founded on the very thoroughgoing
physical realism of men in community. A much more
serious claimant for being a formative influence is the
hermetic literature which emerged in tangible form in
Egypt in the second century AD (note the earlier section
on the dating of the gospel). Here we have an amalgam

of platonism, stoicism, and the mystery religions of the Near East. Again, however, similarities are more apparent than real, and there is in fact a closer relationship between the language of John and the Greek old testament—the Septuagint—than there is between him and the *Hermetica*. To suppose an influence on John one has to presuppose a hypothetical earlier form, whereas it now seems more likely that if anything the influence is the other way round. Still more likely is that there are common sources—the whole religious atmosphere of the eastern Mediterranean and the near Orient going back for centuries—lying in different ways behind each.

This brings us to the question of the influence of judaic thought on John's gospel. There is in fact more direct reference to the fulfilment of old testament prophecies and situations in John than in the synoptics. This is not obvious at first sight because the latter actually quote the old testament far more readily than John does as witness to the way in which it is fulfilled by Jesus. John, however, is saturated through and through with old testament salvific categories, showing Jesus as bringing them to completion. Jesus, for example, is presented as messiah, servant of Yahweh, king of Israel. Also strong and prominent in the gospel are the themes of Genesis, Exodus and Deuteronomy, to name but the most prominent.

It is interesting to note that linguistic parallels suggest that John's knowledge of the old testament is for the most part Palestinian (related to the Palestinian *Targums*) rather than of the diaspora, and this relates it to the literature with which it shows more affinity than with any other—that of the Qumran scrolls. This belongs to an essene community (one of the judaic sects distinct, for example, from the pharisaic and sadducean sects) living near the Dead Sea; and it is all demonstrably earlier than the actual writing of the gospels. Here is to be found a developed theology, manifestly Hebraic, in which prominent features are a modified dualism expressed in terms of the struggle between light and darkness, and a strong sense of sectarian solidarity—both features which emerge, though not in identical form, in John. It was the discovery of these scrolls which clinched the argument, already growing in strength before then, that John is essentially the product of a Palestinian development of the judaic/Hebraic tradition. In the light of this the earlier theories of the predominance of Greek or mandaean influence, and the suggestion that the fourth gospel was only belatedly adapted to fit in with christianity, can be seen all the more clearly to be hypotheses ungrounded in any genuine evidence. In turn this strengthens the growing realisation, already referred to, that there is an eye-witness tradition behind John every bit as authentic as that behind the synoptics.

There are a number of important themes running through the fourth gospel over which scholars have been quarrelling ever since a really critical approach to scripture began. They include John's understanding and awareness of the church as community, and his reference to and presentation of its sacramental life. And there are similar problems about the nature of his eschatology.

Often the particular interpreter's presuppositions on the origin and purpose of the gospel have forced him into what, in retrospect at any rate, can be seen to be serious false judgment. For example, failure to use the terminology used by the synoptics or by Paul does not indicate the absence of the idea in John. Equally, silence (eg on the 'eucharistic institution') cannot demonstrate ignorance; it might equally indicate that the subject is so prominent as to be taken for granted. Without any exaggeration and partisanship it is possible to see in John a sense of the church as community, and the sacraments as radical to that community, expressed in a way which is simply different from that found in other parts of the new testament; and it is possible to see this difference as expressing something complementary rather than contradictory.

Throughout the fourth gospel there is a strong sense of the importance of personal faith in Jesus. This is the criterion by which the true christian is judged. Everything in the gospel is focused around the person of Jesus in an intensive and dramatic way unequalled in the synoptics; and where the synoptics talk about the presence of the kingdom of God, or refer, for example, to the true vineyard of Israel, these are personalised by John with the emphasis on Christ as king, or as the vine. Equally in the fourth gospel the eschatology—the sense of the final age, when all is fulfilled—is richer than in the synoptics and the Pauline literature because it has greater dimensionality: it is not only something in the future, but has already arrived; it does not simply have a horizontal dimension, but a vertical one—heaven and earth are joined together, the physical is fully related to the spiritual.

One cannot argue from these features that John is advocating an exclusive primacy of the individual's relationship to Jesus over against solidarity in assembly— or, in other words, that the concept of the church as corporately the people of God has been superseded by the entirely spiritual acceptance of Jesus as saviour. Nor can one argue that God's gift of faith to the individual fulfils and completes his historical relevance to the world. Such an approach to John is a restricted view from narrow presuppositions which are not supported by evidence from the gospels; it misses altogether the richness which is being offered.

What is happening in the fourth gospel would seem to be that the church life, sacramental and ethical, experienced and lived by the group within which it was developing and finally emerged, is constantly being referred back to Jesus himself in his actual life of communion with his disciples, and of conflict with 'the Jews'. He is the source which gives it meaning; he is the point in which heaven and earth are joined and in which God's promises are fulfilled. It is from Jesus in his ministry that the tradition embodied in the gospel flows forward, and the life of the christian group which embodies it is precisely life in as far, and only in as far, as faith in Christ is its character and quality through and through.

Symbolic representation of the relationship of God to men in Christ is empty and void if it is not an expression of, and an actualisation of, that faith. The mere repetition of Christ's words and actions is in danger of becoming empty symbol rather than living sacrament, if it is not focused on the full depth of what Jesus both said and did; and this depth is at once material and spiritual. Likewise the existence of a church is nothing unless it is an expression of a life of response to Jesus himself, perpetuated in his name and with his living presence. These are the perspectives which emerge in this gospel once one has seen how it is genuinely a gospel in the same sense as the other three are, and once one has seen how it is, in its theological development, a continuation of the development of the consciousness of the history of Israel, which has been taken through the physical, historical, and at the same time infinite 'point' of Jesus of Nazareth.

Style and structure

It should now be easy to see how appropriate the style of the fourth gospel is to the message which it is trying to present. For the greater part its language is at least quasi-poetical, and its form dramatic. It is only in cultures in which rationality has become overdeveloped, at the expense of its origin in the living things which we encounter, that poetry has ever come to be regarded as less real than rational argument and empiric fact. The language and thought of the gospel according to John is close enough to its Hebraic roots to have a strong sense of the power of material reality and of its symbolic extension in poetic form.

Poetry and drama are what turn the 'merely factual' into living actuality. From the point of view of the reconstruction of a 'life of Jesus' the fourth gospel may be a rather unsatisfactory source; but the way in which it presents and structures his key actions and sayings brings out their dramatic relevance in an unparalleled way. What the fourth gospel does to the reader who is already committed in faith is to give him not just the facts— though to these it would seem to be no less committed— but the living actuality of God's saving work for us in Christ.

There are many patterns visible in the way in which the fourth gospel is constructed, some of which are thematic, some symbolic. But the clearest and most significant patterns emerge when one sees how closely tied in with the dramatic form of presentation of its content is the gospel's overall structure.

One way in which the gospel has been divided is according to the number of times that Jesus is presented as going up to Jerusalem. Another scheme, a rather more helpful one, is based on a pattern which can be seen to follow fairly closely its prefigurement in the prologue:

1:35–4:42	The new creation
4:43–6:71	The life of the world
7:1–9:41	The light of the world
10:1–12:50	Rejection by his own people
13:1–20:29	'Reward' of those who believe

The final section here is rather forced, and it is much better in fact to treat this whole section (it consists of eight chapters) as a distinct division of the work over against all (except for the prologue) that goes before it. The gospel thus readily divides into two halves with a prologue at the front and an epilogue at the end. The first part consists in what one might call the public ministry. It is concerned with Christ's miracles, his public teaching, and the growing hostility of the Jews which this arouses. The second half is concerned with his passion and resurrection, or in other words what the evangelist consistently refers to as his glorification. These two main sections have considerable similarities, from the point of view of literary treatment, but they also have considerable differences, which arise from their overall concern and material.

The first part—Christ's ministry—can equally be divided up in several ways. It is possible to use the first parts of the division shown above, though this now becomes even more artificial, and it is more instructive to divide it up on the basis of the gospel's 'historical' progression, thus:

1:19—51	The opening days of the revelation
2–4	Varying responses to Jesus' ministry
5–10	Jesus and the feasts of the Jews
11–12	Jesus moves towards his death and glory

This sort of division, however, despite its usefulness, ignores one of the most salient features of the fourth gospel, and is thus not the best basis for its presentation.

The whole structure and presentation of the gospel (including the second part, though in a slightly different way) is based on a series of incidents (mostly miraculous) in Jesus' ministry. These are chosen for their significance, and this is brought out by the dramatic dialogue (probably partly constructed, partly based on Jesus' traditional sayings) which surrounds the incident. Often this is completed by a summarising monologue. The gospel is thus presented in a series of scenes, each incident with its commentary forming a unit; and of course these then progress according to some such plan as the ones mentioned above. The trouble, however, is that due to rewriting and editing the different types of division no longer fit consistently together.

The first part of the gospel is thus based on a series of 'signs'—significant incidents, in which the significance is spelled out—and has been aptly called *The Book of Signs*. It is an articulated description of Jesus' presentation of himself before men, and is thus also to be seen as representing his public ministry. There is a clear dividing line between this and what follows, for the first part is concluded with a summary statement (12:37–43) to which is characteristically attached a 'farewell' public proclamation (12:44–50). This, then, completes the actual ministry; it brings to a close the self-presentation of Jesus, his acceptance by his disciples and his rejection by 'the Jews'.

The second part takes up from here not only the 'story', but the presentation of the full mystery of God's work amongst men; it goes deeper into what is involved as well as further into the history of the events. The pattern is still in a sense similar. There is this time only one 'incident', though it is a complex one—the death and resurrection together forming Christ's glorification. Also, this time, the 'commentary' (consisting of the farewell discourse, chs 14–17) precedes, of necessity, the action to which it is related.

Then there is another difference. The earlier discourses were public and the signs which were associated with them were in a sense clear and obvious. This final discourse is private, involving only the apostles; and the sign is essentially a 'contradiction'. The discourse itself is full of this 'contradiction': Jesus is leaving them, yet he will not leave them; they cannot see the Father, yet he is showing them the Father. The fullness of the mystery revealed in faith and glorification is beginning to defy explanation, yet it is being presented here in all its fulness, the light and darkness embracing each other in a closer dialectic. It is only in the prologue that what is involved can be stated more succinctly—yet this carries with it a danger of misrepresentation, which is what now has to be avoided.

Book list

Amongst the following books those marked with a single asterisk are recommended with certain reservations. R. E. Brown's magisterial work in two volumes is recommended without hesitation; it is a work of immense scholarship and sanity. The present author wishes to acknowledge a debt of gratitude to this work; he has relied on it considerably in producing his commentary. The works not marked are not necessarily recommended, but contain material which is discussed in these pages.

1. C. K. Barrett, *The Gospel according to St John* (1956).
2. **R. E. Brown, *The Gospel according to John* (1970).
3. R. Bultmann, *The Gospel of St John* (1969).
4. *O. Cullmann, *Early Christian Worship* (1953).
5. *C. H. Dodd, *Interpretation of the Fourth Gospel* (1953).
6. *C. H. Dodd, *Historical Tradition in the Fourth Gospel* (1963).
7. F. R. Hoare, *The Original Order and Chapters of St John's Gospel* (1944).
8. E. Hoskyns, *The Fourth Gospel* (1947).
9. J. Jeremias, *Eucharistic Words of Jesus* (1966).
10. *J. Marsh, *The Gospel of St John* (1968).
11. **J. A. T. Robinson, *Twelve New Testament Studies* (1962).
12. *R. Schnackenburg, *The Gospel according to St John* (1968).
13. W. Temple, *Readings in St John's Gospel* (1952).

1
Testimonies to Jesus
Jn 1:1-51

The prologue

The first, and introductory, chapter of the fourth gospel seems to divide easily into two parts, first the prologue (1–18), and then two incidents in which testimony is borne to Jesus, first by John the Baptist (19–34) and then by the disciples whom Jesus called to him, and especially by Nathanael (35–51). So distinctive is the first part— the prologue—that it is normally treated in its own right, leaving what follows to be considered along with the remainder of the gospel. Such a division is in fact an oversimplification; despite its special and remarkable nature the prologue is not so distinct from the rest of the chapter as first it would appear to be. More than once throughout its course references to John the Baptist keep intruding, and they have marked continuity with what immediately follows.

In fact, more than any other part of the work, the prologue shows signs of the history of the gospel's emergence and development. Roughly speaking it can be seen to consist of three parts, and these, together with their welding into a whole, represent at least three, and quite possibly four, periods in the development of the tradition. (See above, pp 7–9).

The divisions are not difficult to spot, though it is not

possible to be sure of their exact location. At the core of the prologue is a hymn to the word probably emerging as a separate entity within the Johannine tradition at some mid-period in its history. It is fairly easily recognisable by its strophic form and its similarity to other hymns to be found within the new testament. Its probable original form is as follows:

1. In the beginning was the Word,
   and the Word was with God,
   and the Word was God.
3. All things were made through him,
   and without him was not anything made that was
       made.
4. In him was life,
   and the life was the light of men.
5. The light shines in the darkness,
   and the darkness has not overcome it.
10. He was in the world,
    and the world was made through him,
    yet the world knew him not.
11. He came to his own home,
    and his own people received him not.
14. And the Word became flesh
    and dwelt among us.

And then, presumably at a later date, possibly before or possibly at the same time as its incorporation into the gospel, there is what one might call a theological commentary on these verses, for example: He was in the beginning with God; We have beheld his glory, glory as from the only Son of the Father, full of grace and truth; the law was given through Moses, grace and truth came through Jesus Christ ... This commentary consists of verses 2, 12, 13, 14b, 16, 17, 18; but it should be noted that one cannot be absolutely certain about the division between original hymn and its later commentary, the latter being grafted so organically on to the former.

And then finally there are the verses concerning the witness of John the Baptist. These are also grafted into the whole in such a way as to make it difficult to be sure about their original form. Nevertheless, when taken together by themselves, they present us with a continuous narrative which flows without difficulty into the remainder of this chapter:

> There was a man sent from God, whose name was John. He came for testimony, to bear witness to the light, that all might believe through him. He was not the light, but came to bear witness to the light. The true light that enlightens every man was coming into the world. John bore witness to him and cried, 'This was he of whom I said, "He who comes after me ranks before me, for he was before me"'. And this is the testimony of John, when the Jews sent priests and levites from Jerusalem . . . (1:6–9, 15, 19.)

Although these earlier verses have obviously been affected by what they have been incorporated into, nevertheless they look as if they, or something very close to them, formed the original opening of the gospel. They are strikingly similar to the opening of Mark, and to the parallel passages in Matthew and Luke, once one has removed the preliminary material. (It is well worth while underlining with different colours in one's bible these separate sections of the prologue.)

It would seem, then, that the fourth gospel originally started with two accounts of witness to Christ—the testimony of John the Baptist, and that of 'an Israelite indeed, in whom is no guile' (1:47). The links between the new situation and that of the old testament are immediately stated; and on this basis the whole of the gospel proceeds. It must have been felt, however, that something more powerful needed saying to introduce the gospel, to give people a deeper insight into what it was all about. At the time of its original appearance a simple beginning, similar to that of Mark, was all that was required, the rest was given by the living context. But as time passes significance is something which needs more and more spelling out.

If our supposition is correct that the hymn to the word and its theological commentary was something which developed also within the Johannine community (cf pp 195 ff, where we return to this subject), then the final editor had to hand the ideal thing for his purpose. (And this is no less true if the commentary comes from his own hand.) The point to notice here, however, is that the hymn and its commentary have the nature of a summing up of the content and significance of the gospel (we have earlier noted considerable parallelism in their structure). The prologue—apart from the passages on John the Baptist—is in fact basically a conclusion to the gospel and to the whole tradition which it represents; it states more succinctly, and in some ways with even greater power and surety, what is its ultimate significance and content.

There are, however, considerable difficulties with regard to the correct understanding of the prologue. The trouble is largely historical. At the time of its composition such an introduction—expressing the significance and content of the gospel—must undoubtedly have been helpful, especially as it expresses the very essence of a tradition which was still being actually lived in a christian community. Very shortly, however, the situation was to change; the living continuity was to become more and more tenuous, and the church was to come more and more under the intellectual domination of the civilisation through which it was rapidly spreading—in other words, under the influence of Greek idealist thought.

Under these conditions it became increasingly easy to look at the prologue with the eyes of platonism and see in it, and thus in the whole gospel following it, an emphasis on an ideal world of mind and spirit divorced from that true materiality which is the world in which we actually live and hand on to one another the mystery of the incarnation. Christ became the saviour hero whose role it was to lift man up out of this world into the next.

Perhaps the most blatant example of this type of thinking is to be found in Augustine's *Confessions* (though he was radically to reverse it in his later, and unfortunately less well known, writings). And it has dominated large areas of theological thought for centuries, distorting and misrepresenting the gospel. With all this behind us it is very difficult to come to the prologue with a fresh mind and to avoid these dangers.

There is, however, one way which might achieve this; and that is to look at the prologue precisely as a *conclusion* to the gospel—one which summarises its content and points its significance. What is needed is to be able to see the prologue as arising out of the gospel; to see it as expressing something about the relationship between God and man, heaven and earth, which depends upon the actual gospel of Jesus Christ as a living reality, both originally, and now amongst those who believe in him. For this reason we are going to consider the prologue further, and more fully, at the end of this commentary, and confine ourselves here to what was probably the original opening of the gospel—the testimonies of John the Baptist, followed by that of the apostles and Nathanael.

In dissecting and 'restoring' the original form of the prologue's constituent parts do we straightforwardly gain in understanding, or do we also lose something in no longer being able to see it in the way in which the final editor wanted it presented? Are we being faithful, in the long run, to the evangelist's intentions in treating it like this?

Jn 1:19–51. Testimonies

(i) Jn 1:19–34. John the Baptist

These two testimonies taken together, which go to make up the rest of the first chapter, should themselves be seen as forming an introduction to the gospel. It is less satisfactory to regard them as the first incidents in the public ministry, though there is a sense in which they are indeed this. The public ministry, however, as presented in John, consists of a series of signs combined with discourse and theological commentary; this opening passage stands outside that structure. Moreover, it represents more than the ministry, it represents the whole of the gospel: its first half is indeed concerned with public confrontation and public witness, but it moves on, in its second episode, to something more personal in the same way as the gospel itself does when it comes to the 'farewell discourse' at the last supper. This introduction also comes to a conclusion with specific reference to Christ's glorification, again echoing the gospel as a whole.

Another feature is that this section, especially in its second episode (the call of the apostles) expresses in condensed form the understanding of Jesus which his disciples slowly and painfully arrived at throughout their association with him. Also the 'trial' which Jesus was to receive at the end of his ministry, which resulted in his condemnation and death, is here presented at its very beginning—the structure is as if of witnesses bearing testimony at a trial. Seeing this as the implication of God's actual presence among men is the result of theological reflection; crude historical facticity is less likely, and could it in any real sense be said to be something truer?

Nevertheless, one does not want to emphasise the theologising at the expense of factual detail; there is evidence which indicates that the basis of what is being handed on here is every bit as venerable as that found in the synoptics. There may also be details, both with regard to John the Baptist and with regard to the calling of the apostles, which are more accurately portrayed here than elsewhere. Fact and theory are radically tied together throughout this gospel—indeed to achieve this must be regarded as one of its major aims.

What is represented in this confrontation with John the Baptist is the eschatological expectation of the Jewish people; and in his witness we have the christian answer to this. This presents us with two aspects to what is being said: first there is what John the Baptist himself might have understood and have meant; and secondly there is what the evangelist is trying to say. Attempting to discern, insofar as is possible, both of these is what is going to help us to achieve that deeper understanding of scripture which is the food of our faith—itself our response to the message.

The introductory phrases (1:6–9, 15) refer to John as 'witness to the light coming into the world'. As we have already seen, this may result from interaction between the prologue and the original opening; but it should be noted that throughout Isaiah, whose prophecies the Baptist is consistently represented as especially fulfilling, the coming of the Lord is expressed in terms of

light—the passage most well known to us being: 'The
people who walked in darkness have seen a great light'
(Is 9:2). Thus the opening phrases (of our supposed
original) very suitably introduce the whole question of
the nature of the messianic fulfilment which is being
witnessed to here. This is, in fact, what the religious
leaders from Jerusalem want to know.

(It should be noted that in what follows it looks, from
the literary critical point of view, as if two separate
accounts, differing relatively little from one another,
have in fact been conflated to produce the story as we
have it. In this case, as in many such cases, knowledge
of the details of this are not really of very much help to
us; but it is a help to realise that awkwardnesses, hesitan-
cies and duplications which we encounter, which could
otherwise be puzzling, are here, and for the most part,
due to such compilation. What it does witness to is the
respect paid, after only a little while, to the sources of the
tradition. Except in important cases, however, this is not
something to which we are going to draw attention
again.)

John is asked whether he is the messiah, or Elijah or
'the prophet'. To his questioners John was obviously
behaving in an 'eschatological manner'—by his call to
repentance and by his baptising he was in effect proclaiming a new era. Which of the expected figures who
were to bring this about did he claim to be?

In this triple question we have an expression of the
Jewish hope which christian theology was to see as being
fulfilled in its entirety by Jesus. The messiah was the
anointed king of the line of David, Elijah represented the
prophetic movement par excellence, and the 'prophet'
stands for a second Moses (see Deut 18:15–18)—thus
representing the law. Christian theology sees Jesus

expressly as messiah, and as fulfilling, in himself, both the law and the prophets (Mt 5:17). It has long been suspected that parts at least of the fourth gospel contain polemic passages against later sectarians of John the Baptist. Here we see John denying that he is any of these figures, and thus we have to be aware of the possibility of its being primarily a theological presentation. Nevertheless coupled to John's denial is the claim that he is by contrast 'the voice of one crying in the wilderness: "Make straight the way of the Lord"'. In the synoptics this role is imputed to him, in John alone is he represented as claiming this role for himself. Again it might seem that this is part of the evangelist's technique of presenting his theological appreciation of what happened, but we now know that the sect living at Qumran thought of themselves precisely in these terms—preparing the way for the coming of God amongst men. This makes it all the more likely that John the Baptist, who shows considerable affinities with the Qumran movement, did in fact represent himself in these terms, and that we are dealing here with a very early strand of tradition.

John's denial of his being Elijah in this passage presents a slight problem, for in the synoptics he is specifically identified with Elijah. There is, however, considerable evidence (see Robinson, *Twelve New Testament Studies*, pp 28–52) to suggest that it was Elijah's second coming that John was under the impression that he was heralding: he saw Jesus as Elijah. The identification of John himself with Elijah is precisely a theological one, the result of seeing (or, if this derives from an actual *logion*—ie an original saying—of Jesus, the result of expressing) the full implications of the way in which Jesus himself was to fulfil the expectation of Israel. Again, we may well be dealing, here in the fourth gospel, with the very earliest and most primitive tradition.

This takes us from what John denies and affirms about himself, to what he affirms about Jesus (1:26–34). First of all, in answer to further questioning, we have a general statement about his relationship to the one whom he is proclaiming (1:26, 27); and then there follows, after what one might call a dramatic punctuation mark (1:28, 29a) specific testimony to Jesus himself—to which is added further commentary (29b–32 & 33, 34).

The general statement brings out several interesting points. These are, however, so closely woven in with what is said in his actual testimony to Jesus, that it is best to consider them thematically rather than point by point. The first theme is that of their interrelationship. John is the precursor, yet the one he is witnessing to is prior to him both in dignity and origin; John only baptises with water, Jesus will baptise with the Spirit. To this must be coupled the theme of the identity of the one who is coming being unknown until it is revealed by John the Baptist.

In many ways John's account and the synoptics' run very close to each other here: the two different sorts of baptism are referred to in both, so is the humility of John before Jesus. But it is interesting to note that the remark about baptising with the Spirit does not occur until right at the end of John's witness (1:33). It looks, there, as if it were a *logion* being preserved; its absence from the reference to John's actual baptising is noteworthy. The whole emphasis is in fact different in John and in the synoptics. In John the emphasis is on the uncertainty with regard to the identity of the proclaimed figure. Neither John the Baptist, nor his public, can recognise him; it is only through God's revelation that Jesus is known, and to declare this is the whole purpose of John's baptising (1:31).

This position carries two implications: on the one hand it witnesses to a current popular theory about the messiah which contrasts with the more normal one, namely that the messiah would be hidden; and on the other hand—in a sense the fulfilment of this—it witnesses to the way in which God's presence to men in Jesus is in fact only perceived by way of witness to him, and in faith.

It should be noted that this emphasis makes it very unlikely, despite what has frequently been asserted, that here in this 'baptismal scene' in John there is any particular reference to the christian sacrament of baptism. Elsewhere in this gospel there is a very close tie between the liturgical/sacramental life of the church and the way in which Christ's teaching and actions are presented, but here in this introductory chapter the themes which dominate are in a sense riding rather higher—though equally no less down to earth—than at the level of such particularity.

With regard to John's assertion that Jesus is one who ranks ahead of him and existed before him, it is easy to assume that here is a reference of a similar kind to that given by the opening words of the gospel in the prologue. Nevertheless this is not necessarily so; for if John really did see Jesus as the re-personification of Elijah, such a remark would come perfectly naturally without having to posit later theological manipulation here—which from a literary critical point of view looks unlikely anyway. How does this relate, however, to the immediately preceding proclamation of Jesus as the lamb of God who takes away the sins of the world (1:29)?

This is the second theme to be found in this passage,

interwoven with what we have just seen. It too needs considering from the two standpoints of what was meant by John the Baptist himself, and what was written into it by the evangelist. It seems probable that for the Baptist 'the lamb who takes away the sins of the world' is the apocalyptic (and highly mythologico-dramatic) lamb who fights against and conquers the evil in the world. This fits in well with what we know, from other sources, about the preaching of John the Baptist; he speaks of the coming wrath, the axe laid to the roots of the tree, and so on (Luke 3:7–9). This represents a concept of the struggle between good and evil in the world which had been developing for some time in Jewish thought and went on developing in the new testament.

The theme of taking upon oneself the sins of the world, however, introduces another dimension; and this is probably where the theology of the evangelist is beginning to take over. There are two possibilities here, which are not exclusive of one another.

There is considerable likelihood that there is an identification of the lamb of God with the suffering servant, the chosen one of God (cf Is 42:1–4, etc). Isaiah (53:7) describes the servant as being 'like a sheep that is led to the slaughter, and like a lamb before its shearers'. Another notable point is that the servant is spoken of as having the spirit of the Lord put upon him (Is 42:1) and in the gospel John the Baptist bears witness that he has seen the Spirit of God, descending as a dove from heaven, and remaining on Jesus. It should be noted that any identification between the suffering servant and the messiah is not something which could be attributed to John the Baptist—even the Qumran community, who emphasised this, saw their suffering in a very different light.

Another train of thought inevitably introduced by John's proclamation and testimony is that which identifies Jesus with the paschal lamb. This is a theme which is strong in the fourth gospel, particularly with regard to the manner and meaning of Jesus' death; and although the paschal lamb was not originally a sacrifice the Deuteronomic tradition had already brought these two ideas together, and this was to be taken up further by christian theology, eg 'Christ our passover has been sacrificed' (1 Cor 5:7). Both the concepts of sacrifice and liberation are deepened by this development.

It should be noted that there is considerable word variation, particularly with regard to 'lamb', throughout these references. This makes positive affirmation with regard to the presence of these ideas not possible. But the way in which these themes are treated throughout the remainder of the gospel makes these tentative affirmations all the more likely.

1. Why is John baptising people?

2. Did he in fact baptise Jesus? Can you take this for granted in this account? If so, what did it mean? Does it mean anything to the writer of the gospel?

3. Was the role of John the Baptist purely historical, or has his role still to be carried on in some way in the life of the church?

(ii) Jn 1:35–51. The first disciples

John the Baptist's designation of Jesus as the lamb of God is repeated again at the beginning of the second section of this introduction (1:36). This is done to link together what is to follow with what has just been said. At the same time, however, 'the next day' (1:35) indicates that a further step in the development is taking place. What is described in what follows is the transference of John's disciples from him to Jesus. Thus the whole structure of what we have here further enlightens the interrelationship between them which we have already commented on. The passage (1:35–42, 43–51) is again divided into two sections which together contain a number of intertwining themes.

The most prominent of these latter is that of the development of consciousness of what Jesus means to his followers. He is called 'rabbi', once in each section; he is acknowledged as messiah, and then as Son of God and king of Israel; and finally he himself introduces the 'title' of Son of Man. Before commenting on these 'titles', however, we want to look at a problem which is raised by this whole passage. We have here an account of the call of the apostles which is in straightforward contradiction with the account given by the synoptics. There the apostles were all called in Galilee by the shores of the lake, here in John they are called at Bethany (1:28) by the Jordan, just north of the Dead Sea. There have, of course, been attempts to harmonise the two accounts, but there are none which are not far-fetched. Considering the way in which the presentation of the disciples' response to Jesus is clearly 'theological' rather than straightforwardly 'narrational' we might be tempted to treat it simply as this and to accept the synoptics' account as what 'actually happened'. But their account, if one stops to consider it, is equally 'theological'. In fact Luke, who is the most 'practical' of the evangelists, shows signs of uneasiness in presenting it, and it is from Acts that we have a very interesting remark corroborating the Johannine account: whilst discussing the question of the election of a new apostle (to replace Judas) Peter insists that he should be 'one of the men who have accompanied us during all the time that the Lord Jesus went in and out amongst us, *beginning from the baptism of John*'. (Ac 1:21, 22.) It looks as if it is possible that some at least of the apostles were called much earlier than is suggested by the synoptics, and that some of them had indeed been disciples of John the Baptist before attaching themselves to Jesus. An important lesson to be learned from this is the closeness with which 'factual reality' and 'theological insight' are interwoven in John's gospel.

Now let us consider the 'titles' which are applied to Jesus within this context, noting that they are thus not meant to be abstractions, but are precisely expressions involving the personal and physical interrelationship of God and man as these become manifest in Jesus through his call and through our accepting and sharing the life which he offers—this is what is being indicated in microcosm in this passage.

The title of rabbi, teacher, appearing twice here (1:38 and 49), could be anachronistic (we have no other evidence for its use in this sense before about 70 AD), but equally it may represent a true historical memory of how Jesus was normally addressed. However, its frequent use in the first half of John (the other gospels hardly use it at all) and its replacement by 'Lord' as a form of address in the farewell discourse, seem to indicate that its significance is primarily theological. This likelihood is strengthened, in the present passage, by the way in which it is associated, through the language used, with the concept of Jesus as the incarnation of divine wisdom. In the prologue this theme is, of course, strongly emphasised; here it is hinted at by the use of phrases like: 'What do you seek?' (1:38) and 'Where are you staying?' (better 'dwelling'), together with such ideas as: people being called, wisdom only being found by those who answer such a call, and its resulting in their going out in their turn to bring others to him (1:41, 43).

Also in this section of the introductory testimony to Jesus we have a representation—though a somewhat truncated one—of the apostles' acknowledgement of Jesus as messiah. Here it is Andrew, not Peter, who is shown as realising this, but Peter is at the same time given the new name which in Matthew (not in all the synoptics, it should be noted) is shown to be the reward for such insight. Here the 'insight' is interestingly attributed to Jesus (1:42). One should note, in passing, that the use of the Aramaic word 'Cephas', alone to be found in this description, would seem to indicate that we have here some of the earliest traditional material.

The basic reason given here for this acknowledgement of Jesus as messiah is that the first two disciples went off with Jesus and stayed with him (1:39). This very brief presentation contains an emphasis which is radical to this gospel, and indeed to the whole authentic christian tradition, namely that it is through sharing life (and this of course means sharing death and resurrection) with Jesus that he is revealed to men in his true nature.

The episode relating to Nathanael, which contains the next set of 'titles', is full of interesting problems; but it would seem to be a pity to concentrate, as has so often been done, on the aspects which are really rather trivial: such for example as who was Nathanael, was he one of the twelve? and what was he doing 'under the fig tree'?

The episode opens with Philip saying to Nathanael 'We have found him of whom Moses in the law, and also the prophets, wrote, Jesus of Nazareth, the son of Joseph' (1:45). Although this does not involve any further 'titles' it certainly does indicate a further stage of development in understanding the role of Jesus. It reflects the way in which the disciples learnt at the time of the resurrection that all that had happened had to be this way, Jesus himself on the road to Emmaus explaining it to them 'beginning with Moses and all the prophets' (Lk 24:27). It may well also link up with the questions put to John the Baptist with regard to Elijah and 'the prophet'. Thus when taken together with Andrew's recognition of Jesus as the messiah, we may have here the affirmative counterpart to John's denial shown at the beginning. Even if John the Baptist did not recognise it, the church, here in the person of the evangelist, recognises that Jesus indeed fulfils all the eschatological expectations and hope of Israel.

Nathanael's reaction is interesting, having two important aspects to it. First of all he reacts in the same way as do so many of those who acknowledge the law and the prophets: 'Can anything good come out of Nazareth?' But, in being further invited, he is willing to go and see; he is not closed in as are 'the Jews' (the scribes and pharisees), but remains open. This is probably the basic reason for his being greeted by Jesus as 'an Israelite indeed, in whom is no guile' (1:47). To presume anything else (except a reference to Jacob/Israel, which may anyway, as an allusion, be reflexive rather than traditional) is purely speculative, and such speculation tends to obscure the point which is being made beyond any other here. This is that Nathanael represents the new Israel, which is precisely constituted by those who come to Jesus. This also is reflected in the prologue where we read: 'He came to his own, but his own received him not. But to all who received him . . . he gave power to become the children of God' (1:11, 12).

Recognising that Nathanael represents the new Israel, some people have suggested that he is in fact purely a figurative concept inserted here by the evangelist. This would also explain his subsequent total 'disappearance' as a person from the gospel narratives. (His 'reappearance' in 21:2 would seem to be more of an artificial reference back to this scene than anything else, though it cannot simply be dismissed on this assumption.) This suggestion is nevertheless entirely forced: however representative Nathanael may be there is nothing to indicate that the people involved in this chapter are anything other than actual human beings; such intrusion would be indicated by a far greater break in literary form than anything to be found here.

What immediately follows this is puzzling. The reference to what Nathanael was doing under the fig tree must have been meaningful to the original readers of the gospel, but for us such meaning is lacking. Speculation is again more or less useless. One should also notice that Nathanael's reaction goes far beyond anything which could be occasioned by a demonstration of second sight by Jesus. His response is emphatically the witness of the entire gospel. Thus the evangelist at this point may only have had this sort of consideration in mind—which brings us back again, however, to the puzzling nature of the reference to the fig tree.

If this detail seems to us to lack meaningfulness, nevertheless it is clear that the titles bestowed upon Jesus here are full of it. Jesus is the Son of God, the king of Israel. These would both seem to be messianic titles, but considering the theological emphasis and the introductory nature of this whole section it is difficult to disassociate this affirmation from the idea of a proclamation of Jesus' divinity. The whole gospel (if we exclude the epilogue) comes to a climactic conclusion with Thomas' similar affirmation of Jesus as 'my Lord and my God' (20:28), and it is interesting to note that the verses which immediately follow in each case have a notable similarity.

The title 'king of Israel' ties in well with the whole train of thought, already seen as being present, which identifies the new Israel with those who come to Jesus. It has been remarked that 'Israel' means 'one who will see God'; thus the affirmation of Jesus as Son of God and as king of Israel fits well on the lips of one whom Jesus has described as an 'Israelite indeed, in whom is no guile'. A whole host of ideas with regard to the nature of Jesus, his mission, his being accepted by those whom he has called, and so on, are woven together in this passage with great density. The living context for the reality of all this is given by Jesus in the words with which he answers Nathanael: 'You will see greater things than these' (1:50); and it is difficult to see this other than as an allusion to what is now to follow: the first main section of the gospel, the 'book of signs and discourses' which constitutes the presentation of Jesus' public ministry, followed by the discourse on, and the achievement of, his glorification.

What appears (from the way in which it is presented) as a separate *logion* (1:51) is attached at this point with extreme appropriateness. There are endless theories about what exactly is meant by, and what exactly are the sources of, this saying. They are probably multiple. Conjoined here are the ideas of the Son of Man and the presence of God in his glory; and the fulfilment of the old covenant in the new and the resultant bridging together of heaven and earth are clearly hinted at. One thing, at any rate, is clear: what is being asserted is that the glory of God has achieved its perfection as something revealing itself to men in the person of Jesus of Nazareth; and what could be a more appropriate ending to the gospel's introduction?

If we have gone into this introduction at fairly considerable length it has been to show two things. The first is the richness of the material here—a richness which is apparent throughout the whole gospel. It is hoped that some indication has been given of the way in which this can be appreciated. The second is the way in which, in this gospel, the theological thought of the evangelist, together with the tradition behind him, is tied in extremely closely with the actual physical reality of what went on in Palestine at the time of Jesus' ministry and his living together with those whom he called. At times the concentration may be on the more 'theological' side; at times we may have a record of material at least as old, or at times even older, than that contained in the synoptic gospels. The gospel of John can in no way be treated as merely later theologising—even of the highest kind—nor is its theology in any way simply abstract; it is, throughout its length, incarnate in its historical origins, and their living continuation. Indeed it may be said—and it is hoped that this may become clear as we proceed—that the purpose of the fourth gospel throughout is at least largely to demonstrate the necessity of this.

1. What relationship can you see between Jesus and his original disciples as depicted in this scene?

2. What difference does it make to realise that some of them at least were probably disciples of the Baptist first?

3. Can we see ourselves, as Christ's disciples, reflected in any way in this scene?

2

The public ministry
Jn 2:1–12:50

Introduction

It has already been admitted that there is a sense in which Jesus' public ministry clearly starts with his baptism by John and the subsequent call of the apostles as recounted in the first chapter. Nevertheless, as we have seen, these incidents are presented, not so much as constituting part of the ministry, but as providing an introduction to the gospel as a whole. The ministry receives its presentation in the chapters that follow; and the first point to notice is that this is precisely a presentation rather than an account. In other words selective material is used, and it is carefully written up in such a way as to bring out, not only its significance, but the significance of the whole of the ministry—indeed ultimately of the whole of Christ's salvific work.

This presentation is based on a series of 'signs', or (for the most part) miracles, which Jesus performed during the course of his ministry. What, however, is most noticeable in comparison with the synoptics is that only a minute fraction of the miracles recorded there are presented by John; they have been particularly chosen, not only for their significance, but because they are especially suitable for presenting the understanding of Jesus which was brought to, and developed within, the primitive christian community from which this gospel eventually emerged.

Further differences between the synoptic and Johannine presentation of Christ's miracles are instructive. John strongly plays down the 'marvellous' element in these incidents; they are not presented, as they are so often in the synoptics, as 'signs and wonders'. The Johannine miracle accounts are much closer to those in the synoptics which indicate the presence amongst men of a new order of things in which God is truly present to his people and is fulfilling his promises to them (consider Jesus' answer to John the Baptist in Mt 11:2–6). In sum Jesus' miracles are presented by the fourth gospel as works that establish God's kingdom and point to its nature.

This ties in interestingly with the way in which the signs (as the miracles are always referred to by the evangelist, the apostles, etc) are spoken of by Jesus as his 'works'. It is not impossible that this represents something of the original recollection of Jesus, but it is certainly not possible to argue to this, for the distinction here and the significance of the usage is specifically theological: to the disciples the works of Jesus are signs through which their faith becomes a reality, to Jesus they are what he does in the name of his Father and are thus what his Father brings about through him. And one could add to this that the emphasis of the term 'work' is on the divine perspective of what is accomplished, whereas that of 'sign' is on its human and psychological effect.

All of this ties in very closely with the way in which the works of Jesus are continually associated with the work of God as portrayed in two particular areas of the old testament: the creation narratives of Genesis, and the liberation of God's people (together with the covenant given to them) as presented in Exodus. There are also strong similarities between the signs and works of Jesus and those in the old testament prophetic movement. In each case further and 'more spiritual' significance is located within a work already carrying its own significance; and this in turn goes towards the actual bringing about of what is signified, though in the case of Jesus this latter aspect is intensified.

Thus we find the 'work' itself and its significance bound together in the closest bond, and the 'explanations' which follow the 'signs' in the discourses built up around them equally fit into this unity. We find Jesus himself presented as saying: 'The *words* that I say to you I do not speak on my own authority; but the Father who dwells in me does his *works*' (14:10). There is, as Dodd puts it, a unity of act and word fundamental to the Johannine philosophy which distinguishes it radically from the abstract intellectualism or mysticism of much of the thought of the time.

It might thus be said that the style in which John presents Christ's ministry is no mere literary artifice for the sake of catechetical effectiveness, but is radical to the understanding of the message which is here being conveyed. This whole characteristic of the gospel is what makes it possible for the presentation of the ministry to be at the same time full of sacramental reference. Not only do the sacraments indicate Christ's presence in the church in the same way as the works of Jesus indicate the Father's presence in him, but they bear a direct relationship to these works as the extension in the church of their living and actual significance.

The account of the public ministry of Jesus is built up, then, from a number of carefully selected signs to which are added, as an extension of the dramatic presentation, appropriate discourses and commentary. So carefully have these been chosen that each incident can, in a sense, be said to contain, and even partially express, the whole of the gospel message—though this does not mean that in each it is fully spelled out. Of its very nature this message is not susceptible to straightforward linear or scalar presentation—it is far too rich for that. Thus the movement of the episodes is complex, and can possibly best be compared with the strands of a musical composition. Themes are introduced, developed, dropped, re-taken up in different relationships; and as this happens they grow in strength and significance.

The episodes, whose themes develop and interrelate in this way with one another, clearly have a common pattern; but their structure is in fact subject to endless variation as again and again Jesus is presented under the different aspects of the way in which he makes God present to men and men to God. They present this as taking place through confrontation and enlightenment, through death and resurrection; and together they lead remorselessly to the climax of the gospel where the implications of faith and fidelity are spelled out in the 'Book of Glory' (chs 13–20.)

Jn 2:1–4:42. The first episodes
(1) Jn 2:1–11; 2:12–25. Cana and the temple

The 'Book of Signs' starts off with a number of incidents and comments which seem, from some points of view, to be rather disjointed—at least with regard to their literary and dramatic structure. The shape which is going to be developed in the gospel is only beginning to form; the relationship between sign and dialogue does not immediately take up the shape which it is to have

later, and although the theological comments are clear
enough it is not always so easy to see exactly to which
signs they are referring. It is also not exactly clear every
time what is meant to be taken as a sign and what is not.

All this lack of exactitude is far from reprehensible;
what we are being presented with is primarily a living
situation, whether theologically articulated or not; to
over-articulate it before it begins to take life would be to
destroy it. This is perhaps why we start off with something
which is in one way sharp and clear, and which is terminated with a brief and hard-hitting comment—the
wedding feast at Cana where Jesus turned the water into
wine.

It is notable that of the seven actual 'miracles' depicted in John, three would appear to be ones also
described in the synoptics, and three more are of a very
similar nature to others in the synoptics; only this miracle
at Cana is without parallel. Of course it has a vague
affinity with the multiplication of loaves (especially
through its eucharistic imagery); nevertheless most of its
features are entirely its own. That it clearly contains
references both to the old testament (eg Melchisedek's
offering to Abraham, Gen 14:18) and to the eucharistic
theology of the church, has made some people think that
it is a symbolic incident invented to depict the changing
of the old covenant, with its emphasis on ritual cleansing,
into the new with its life achieved and communicated
in the blood shed on the cross and handed on sacramentally in the church.

It would be difficult to deny that these elements are
there (and indeed it is far from our wish to do so) but
what should be noted is that this will hardly do as an
explanation, and certainly not as a full explanation, of
the passage. Equally, however tempting it is to see the

influence of such elements, it cannot be explained by reference to pagan mythological rites connected with the wine harvest. This is so for two reasons.

First, and we will return to this shortly, the emphasis put on this incident by the evangelist is quite distinct, and is on a totally different aspect of it; and as a result one cannot assert anything beyond a reference to these themes. The second point is that there is too much explicit detail, and un-tidied-up detail at that, for it easily to be a literary invention. Although it is clearly symbolic in several ways, and equally full of practical problems, it has the general taste of an authentic incident, in much the same way as the passages on John the Baptist and the calling of the apostles which we have already seen.

In order to get a little closer to the incident's significance it is worthwhile bringing together a diversity of points here. It is emphasised (2:11) that this was the first sign that Jesus performed. Also, as we have already seen in the preceding chapter, there are discrepancies between the Johannine and the synoptic descriptions of the calling of the apostles, and we are not able to dismiss the former in favour of the latter. This present incident could well have taken place very early on in Jesus' public ministry before all the twelve were actually gathered together. There are indeed many aspects of the way in which it is told—the location, the family presence, the nature of the occasion—which make this likely.

This, however, raises a problem. Assuming that Mark's gospel is based on Peter's preaching (which, although generally taken for granted, cannot be regarded as certain) it might seem odd that such an incident is not recorded there, especially if Peter had already joined Jesus by that time. But it must be remembered that Mark is almost as selective of its incidents as is John, and if the theological significance of an incident is not clear, or in other words if it does not fit into the patterns of thought of a tradition which might otherwise have transmitted it, its chances of preservation are far from being good. It is not unlikely that it was only within the Johannine tradition that such significance was clear. Indeed its eucharistic echoes and its theme of the old being transformed into the new were aspects which would encourage its preservation within the Johannine environment, but the one point which is outstandingly emphasised—the lesson which we are meant to take away—is that it is through his signs that Jesus manifested his glory and that belief in him grew (2:11). The inclusion of this miracle in the gospel would appear to be basically because it was the *first* of these signs.

Other things are to be learned once we have got this perspective right. First of all we can consider how exactly it was that this particular miracle revealed Jesus' glory. The most obvious reason is the plenitude of messianic reference which is to be found here. A wedding itself, given the right conditions, is a messianic symbol; it is used in Isaiah to indicate God's final redemptive intervention (cf Is 62:4, 5). The steward's remark 'You have kept the good wine until now' is equally indicative of the fact that something new, and life giving, is at hand. The remarkable quantity of water turned into wine (about 120 gallons) must be connected with the same sort of symbolism used when Jesus talks, with hyperbole, about the seed bringing forth fruit fifty and a hundredfold (Lk 8:8)—and both passages are clearly eschatological when seen in the light of prophetic statements (cf Hos 14:7; Am 9:13, 14).

Then there is the relation of the old which is passing

away to the new which is at hand, which has already
been mentioned. Mary's 'they have no wine' can easily
be seen as a comment on the ultimate value of the ritual
purifications—there is no real life in them; and the wine
coming from these very jars indicates continuity on the
one hand and the difference between the past and the
future on the other. There also seem to be hints here of
the wisdom motive (to be taken up more fully later).
Wisdom prepares a banquet, asking men to drink from
her wine (Sir 15:3; 24:19, 21), and in this act she
bestows upon them her message (faith).

A further point which should be made is that despite
many attempts to do so it is impossible to derive any
positive elements of a Marian theology from this incident.
The conversation between mother and son—which is
clearly not a rebuke or rebuttal—would seem to indicate
the point at which Jesus' ministry springs forth from his
home and family environment, though the pattern of
request, apparent refusal, perseverance and compliance
is something which recurs in other contexts. But this
concept of the incident witnessing to the emergence of
Jesus' ministry is reinforced by the emphasis on its
being the first sign that Jesus performed. One should also
note, however, that there is a tendency in Johannine
theology to depict Mary as representing the motherhood
of the church over the faithful. This theme is to occur
again at the crucifixion and is prominent in Revelation.

With no more than the single comment which we have
referred to (2:11) and a 'stage reference' which associates
Jesus and his disciples with his family (2:12), the scene
changes to Jerusalem at passover time and we are presented with John's account of the cleansing of the temple.
Here two totally different problems confront us: first
there is the discrepancy between this account and that

of the synoptics, and second there is the vexed question whether this incident is meant to indicate another sign or not. This latter is probably something one can see both ways; there is a way in which this incident is complementary to the Cana miracle, filling in the significance of Christ's life as a whole which is not indicated there. The symbolism of the old being replaced by the new is clearly continued, so is the comment on the state of the old order: the Father's house has been turned into a house of trade (2:16).

At the same time, however, this deed is clearly one of Jesus' 'works', for it both achieves something definite— altering the relationship between himself and the officials of Judaea—and is full of messianic significance (2:17). Because they are blind 'the Jews' cannot see this, seeing only the affront to themselves, and ask precisely for a sign to justify his actions. We are meant to see the irony of this, for of course the sign has already been given, so what they now receive is its further significance: the temple is indeed to be done away with but it will not really be destroyed, rather it is fulfilled in Jesus himself by his resurrection—in his own body.

The problem of the discrepancy between John's account of Jesus' action in the temple and that of the other gospels is of interest, but not because we feel there is any particular need to reconcile their chronologies—they are not presenting us with a 'life of Christ', but rather with the life which is Christ's. The interest lies in the light which is thrown on the mind of the evangelist and the way in which he is trying to present the gospel. Nevertheless chronological aspects do have significance with regard to this; it is interesting that what is clearly the same incident is described here at the beginning of Christ's ministry whilst in the synoptics it is presented as taking place just after his triumphal entry into Jerusalem before his crucifixion. This latter would seem to be the more logical position: we can hardly imagine such an action being allowed to take place twice, and it was such an affront that it made the authorities determine to do away with its perpetrator, which is how the synoptics present it.

Nevertheless things are not quite as simple as that; there are some not insignificant pieces of evidence which suggest that the Johannine chronology might be the more accurate, and some of the most important commentators have argued to this effect. There is, for example, the reference to John the Baptist in the synoptic account of the incident (cf Mk 11:27, 28) which would indicate a relatively early dating; and when the witnesses at Jesus' trial testify about his threatening to destroy the temple one gets the impression that this is not a threat which has only just been made.

These problems are resolved when one realises the possibility of this incident being compounded of two chronologically disparate elements; but the question then becomes one of why John has attached a later incident to what is probably an earlier saying and presented them to us at precisely this point. Now there is interestingly some evidence that there has been an editorial shift here: later in the gospel the reason given for the Jews determining to put Jesus to death is the raising of Lazarus from the dead. This, as we shall see later, looks like additional editorial matter introduced from the tradition into the gospel after it had first taken literary form. It may be that this material has in effect displaced the original reason—the cleansing of the temple—which was then transferred to this earlier setting.

Its transference to this particular point would seem

to have a number of reasons. First, it is associated here, as in the synoptics, and presumably in its first Johannine location, with the presence of Jesus in Jerusalem at a passover. Secondly, as we have seen, it ties in closely with what has already been presented, though we should note that this whole supposition makes it less likely that it is meant to be understood in any way as one of Jesus' 'signs' and more likely that it effectively forms part of the theological commentary—though this line of argument should not be taken too far because of what follows in chapter 3.

John only quotes half a verse of Ps 69 in reference to Jesus' action, but it is worth considering the possibility that a wider reference is meant, especially seeing how well what precedes and follows fits in with what the gospel is here depicting:

> I have become a stranger to my brethren,
>   an alien to my mother's sons.
> For zeal for thy house has consumed me,
>   and the insults of those who insult thee have
>   fallen upon me. (Ps 69:8, 9)

If this is to be understood the whole incident links up together with remarkable strength, and the factors of belief and disbelief, of continuity with the old testament and its being supplanted in Christ—all of which led to his death and resurrection—are brought out more forcefully in the whole incident. As suggested earlier, even if it is not fully spelled out, each incident in John's gospel contains, in a remarkable way, the whole of that gospel.

This discussion has thrown light on one of the most interesting aspects of the literary/theological construction of the fourth gospel. Mention has already been made a

number of times of the way in which significant actions of
Jesus have been chosen to form the articulatory points of
the gospel's presentation of his ministry; these are then
followed by discourses spelling out the significance. Here
we are beginning to see this process in action—the
relevant discourses are still to come in chapters 3 and 4—
but at this moment we can also see another important
element: other actions in Jesus' life, which are particularly rich in meaning, are 'pulled in' to help form the
theological commentary on the basic incident—we are
going to see the same sort of thing happening in chapter
4.

Chapter 2 concludes with a few verses (23–25) which
form another 'dramatic punctuation mark'—a comma,
or semicolon. The main point of this passage is to link
the incident which has just been narrated with the
following discourse which is focused on Nicodemus—a
man who believed, though only in a partial way. But
at the same time it does introduce something of its own.
Clearly, although the signs referred to here may well
have been, or are likely to have been, miracles performed
by Jesus, they are not signs in the sense of those which
articulate this whole section of the gospel. These latter
are precisely the revelation—the actual presentation and
acceptance—of God's glory in Jesus (2:11); the former
are seen as only partially this, at best; they indicate something closer to the presentation of Jesus' miracles in the
synoptic gospels, and it looks as if this is an independent part of the overall tradition taken up and used to
effect in this context. It refers, if only obliquely, to
the way in which men can see and yet not see (cf Mk 4:
12; Jn 12:40), and to the way in which the deeds in
which Jesus manifests himself divide men for and against
him.

1. Is it purely artificial to link together as 'one sign' the wedding at Cana and the cleansing (and destruction) of the temple?

2. Is the eucharist a wedding feast?

3. How is the eucharist related to Christ's ministry as opposed to his passion?

(ii) Jn 3:1–21; 22–36. Nicodemus and John the Baptist

The whole question of what part was played by Nicodemus in Jesus' life as one of his disciples is left completely vague by John, though he is referred to twice more in such a way as to leave little doubt that he was indeed a real person having a real, if ambiguous, relationship to Jesus. Here in the first part of this chapter (Jn 3:1–21) he is simply being used by the evangelist for his theological and literary purposes, though characteristically this would seem, from such references as that in Jn 7:50, to be based on an actual incident. The synoptic gospels do not mention Nicodemus at all however.

Once again the question of chronological exactitude is of interest so long as we do not get hooked up by it but treat it as a means for better understanding the evangelist's mind. The incident certainly seems to have been 'misplaced' from a narrow historical point of view; it would fit in far better just after Nicodemus' statement to his fellow pharisees later on in the gospel (Jn 7:50). But placing it here in the gospel has considerable advantages from the author's point of view. In the situation depicted and developed (in chapter 2), which contains elements both of a sign which induced faith in its witnesses and a confrontation with the authorities and representatives of the established religion, it is obviously of advantage to have Jesus 'cross-examined' by one who, at least in some ways, bridges the gap.

With regard to the content of the discourse Nicodemus, as can be seen (3:2, 4, 9), simply provides the cues for Jesus to hold forth and proclaim the truth—or at least that is how it appears at first glance. The problem which immediately arises, however, is whether it is Jesus who is talking or the evangelist. There are certainly elements which indicate that it is not actually Jesus who is speaking: for example 3:3 and the verses which follow depend for their effect on a play of words which only makes sense in Greek (being 'born anew' could as well be rendered as 'born again' or as 'born from above'; Nicodemus understands it in the first sense, but Jesus interprets it in the second); 3:11 seems to be the church speaking rather than Jesus, and so on.

Does this suggest that the whole discourse is put into Jesus' mouth by the evangelist, and is an expression of the theology of this latter rather than anything Jesus himself might have said? To insist on this would be to go beyond the evidence, and there are sufficient parallels with material in the synoptic tradition to suggest that there are also considerable elements of traditional matter throughout this discourse (cf Introduction, pp 5–11). It looks as if a nucleus of traditional material has been used here in very much the same way as any preacher at any time will incorporate such material in his presentation of Christ and his gospel. It is not much use, under such circumstances, attempting to extract words which could actually have come from Jesus' lips—though in some other contexts this is a perfectly feasible thing to do. What we can, however, be almost certain of here, as in the other discourses, is that they are not simply the intellectual invention of a later age, but rather the developed expression—having direct continuity with it—of what actually took place in Jesus' ministry.

This discourse has an obviously deliberate structure. The first point to notice is how it is a rounded whole: at the beginning Nicodemus comes to Jesus in the dark; at the end we are told that we have to leave the darkness and come into the light. There is a similar 'inversion' in the actual structure also: at the beginning Nicodemus says, 'Rabbi, we know you are a teacher come from God' (3:2); then eight verses later, at a critical turning point, Jesus says, 'Are you a teacher of Israel and yet you do not understand this? . . . we speak of what we know' (3:10). These two sayings mark the progression of the argument from the first half of the discourse, concerned with the necessity of being born anew, to the second half which presents us with the 'way' in which this is achieved, namely through belief in the Son, which brings men into the light, and is effective precisely on account of the return of the Son to the Father.

In order to appreciate what is being said in this discourse we have to look at it in two different ways; first of all there is the superficial (which does not mean unprofound) level of the conversation as actually presented, and secondly there are the implications which must have been seen, and were meant to be seen, by its original readers. With regard to the first we see a characteristic use of Johannine irony: Nicodemus misunderstands both what Jesus is and what he says to him, and this allows Jesus (and/or the evangelist speaking on his behalf) to transfer the whole dialogue from one plane on to another. Nicodemus recognises Jesus as coming from God (3:2), but Jesus has to explain that the way he comes from God was not quite what Nicodemus was thinking—hence the whole conversation about rebirth, where again we get ambiguity and misunderstanding. This leads to the discussion of the Spirit and how one is in fact begotten of the Spirit. At this primary level the word is particularly important; despite the Hebrew for 'spirit' being feminine (and the Greek neuter) the spirit is seen as the engendering principle here: as life comes from the father's seed, so heavenly life comes through the Father giving his Spirit.

This is taken up more fully in the second half of the discourse (3:10–21), but at this point (3:5, 6 & 8) we are offered more on the nature of the Spirit—it is as indeterminable as the wind, and yet as vital as is breath—the word-play here has a number of different depths. One should notice how radically continuous the language here is with the old testament prophets; Isaiah, Joel and Ezekiel are each brought to mind, with their talk of the outpouring of the spirit. One should also notice the nature of the Johannine distinction between flesh and spirit which is brought up here for the first time and is implicit throughout the passage (and explicit in 3:6): it is quite different from the much later distinction between body and soul, or between material and spiritual as found in both Greek and gnostic thought. The contrast is between those who are simply 'sons of man' (ie mortal) and those who are 'sons of God', or in other words between man as he is and man who is led to the Father in the Spirit through believing in, and sharing the life of, Jesus.

This leads us straight into part two of the discourse (3:10–21) which is in fact straightforwardly a speech by Jesus—Nicodemus would seem to exist silently during its course. But before he goes his question 'How can this be?' (3:9) is answered. It can only be brought about by someone whose origin is in heaven, but has come amongst men and will lead them back to his Father (3:13). Here we have echoes (or pre-echoes) of the doctrine contained in the prologue. The emphasis here, however, is on faith, and disbelief is put into relief over against this; and this faith is shown to be related to the significance of, and light shed on the world in, Christ's death by crucifixion (3:14, 15).

The final verses of Christ's speech (3:16–21) are a general conclusion which in slightly differing form (though with considerable parallelism) is repeated again and again (eg 3:31–36; 12:44–50): life and death, faith and disbelief, light and darkness, are all contrasted and related, and this is set in the context of the love of God who gave his only Son so that men might become the sons of God.

Now we have to examine the question of what is also to be implicitly understood in this whole passage (3:1–21). The main item which draws attention here and does not seem to be explained in itself is the mention of water, which is connected with the gift of the Spirit (3:5). Is this to be read as a clear reference to christian baptism by which men are reborn and enter into the life of faith? Some have suggested that it was added only in the final redaction and indicates a move from a non-sacramental to a sacramental outlook, but there is no evidence at all for this, and it is wholly hypothetical. It is certainly the only mention of water, or anything like it, here, but the messianic and eschatological prophecies of the old testament often link the outpouring of the Spirit with water, so it would not seem to be out of place on any score; but equally its inclusion does not seem to be necessitated by the flow of the argument.

A baptismal interpretation forces a change from the idea of being begotten by the spirit to that of being born of the spirit, but this is an accommodation easily made.

It is in fact extremely hard to come down one way or another on this point from the evidence of the text itself; there is however one external factor which would seem to make it more than likely that the whole passage is meant to be taken in a sacramental as well as in a doctrinal way. This is the deliberate tacking on of the passage on John the Baptist which immediately follows. It may well be that the original matter upon which this whole discourse was built up had no actual sacramental baptismal significance, but the community within which this discourse was preached soon realised how close the link was and understood it in this way. One is not able to say anything more than this; and it is certainly not possible to argue to the necessary connection between the use of water and the outpouring of the Spirit. Nevertheless the close interrelation of these two would seem to fit in well with the overall Johannine mentality which welds 'fact' and 'further significance', deed and symbolism, so closely together into a dynamic and living whole.

The main interest of the passage which immediately follows on John the Baptist (3:22–30) is the light it throws on the construction and genesis of the gospel. Here we have an example of one of those many passages in John where the sequence is awkward and looks superficially as if something had got in the wrong order or somehow muddled up—there is an awkwardness of linkage in style and in matter. With regard to the latter the whole of this passage looks as if it belongs originally to the same sort of material as that concerning John the Baptist in chapter 1.

Some people suggest that the original scene has been divided up and the contents of chapters 2 and 3 inserted in between. But this would not seem to be the case because there would be an equal lack of logical construction and follow-through if they were put together. It looks much more as if this particular passage were additional traditional material about that first meeting which has been incorporated into the gospel during the later stages of its development for a particular purpose. As has just been suggested there seems a considerable likelihood of this purpose having been to accentuate the baptismal significance of the conversation with Nicodemus. That this is not a result of the final redaction, but an earlier editing and developing, would seem to be clear from the fact that the quite different hand of the final redactor can be discerned in 3:24.

The final words of John the Baptist also seem to sum up the transition from the old to the new which has been a constant feature of the incidents which we have been looking at in chapters 2 and 3. They lead quite conveniently into the final speech (3:31–36) which probably comes from the evangelist himself, or else possibly from traditional material deriving from Jesus, which is once more a summary—probably another version of what we saw in 3:16–21. This time, however, there is more emphasis on the relation of the Father to the Son and on how, by believing in Jesus, we are caught up in this and this leads us to eternal life.

Can one say that, whereas the old law was designed to cope with man as he is, Christ offers him the promise of his fulfilment, ie the perfection of what he could be? Does this distinction cover that between 'worldly' and 'spiritual' as understood by John?

(iii) **Jn 4:1–42. The Samaritan woman**

Here we have another startling example of the way in which John combines detailed incident, with considerable local colour, together with profound theological discourse in a way which produces something far richer than either straightforward biography or theological statement. The structure is complex; the encounter, the departure and arrival of the disciples and so on, are inter-woven with simple dialogue, and in this are inserted a number of short but powerful set speeches. Although the incident contains a 'miracle' which induces belief in the woman—a clairvoyance similar to that reported as affecting Nathanael (1:48–49)—this is not in any way presented as one of Jesus' signs; indeed it is pointed out that full faith came to the people of the woman's village only as a result of Jesus going and staying with them (4:40–41). The whole incident is presented as a dramatic discourse which reflects back on and comments on Jesus' ministry as so far depicted; it closes this section and brings the ministry to its second phase of presentation—Jesus in Galilee.

One of the things to be noted is the accuracy of detail and verisimilitude achieved in the whole presentation. The author clearly knows (either from personal knowl-edge or accurate tradition) the details of the place and the views which would have been held by such a Samari-tan woman. So far, although totally uncorroborated by other evidence, the incident looks as if it were based on traditional material of some detail. A great deal of the conversation has a similar ring; it is only some parts of what Jesus says that are set-pieces of theological commentary.

The scene divides into two: firstly Jesus' encounter with the Samaritan woman (4:4–26), and secondly the ensuing conversation with the returned disciples (4:27–38); the last few verses (4:39–42) provide an important conclusion whose import has already been mentioned. In the first scene we have all the usual 'tricks' of ambiguity and irony and the transference of meaning from one level to another. One should notice a possible reference to the crucifixion in the assertion that it was at the sixth hour that Jesus asks the woman to give him a drink (4:7; cf 19:14, 28)—though this is somewhat tenuous. Another point similarly worth noting is that Jesus seems ready to acknowledge to this woman that he is the messiah; here is something quite different from the reticence he shows in the presence of 'the Jews'. The latter are what one might call his 'professional enemies' whilst the woman is only accidentally so as the result of a history which has now passed on and is no longer relevant (cf 4:21–24).

There are two main themes in this first scene: firstly that of living water, secondly that of God as Spirit. The dialogue starts on the misunderstanding of the phrase 'living water' (4:10). The woman thinks he means flowing (ie spring) over against flat (well) water. There is no mention of this well in the old testament, but there is a tradition about the well of Jacob at Haran that when he uncovered it the well flowed up and went on flowing like a spring for some time—hence the (to us ironic) reference to 'our father Jacob' (4:12). Jesus' answer is a proclamation that he is talking about the very essence of life, not about trivia, he is the source of life. Of course the water is not the life itself, but bestows that life by being drunk (4:14); John's imagery is never cut off from the very stuff of earthly reality—the vitality, here, of water in a hot and arid country. There are two major themes connected with water which seem to be indicated here. First of all there is a close association between flowing water, and drinking one's fill of it, and the presence amongst men of God's wisdom (cf Prov 13:14; 18:4, Is 55:1, Sir 24:21–29). In the last of these references

God's wisdom is identified with the law (the *torah*),
which interestingly fits in with the whole argument on
worship and the law between Jesus and the woman, and
her expectation of a prophet (to be identified, by development, with her concept of messiah—almost certainly
non-Davidic, but representing a second Moses, 4:19, 25).

The second theme with regard to water is that which
associates it with the Spirit and its presence amongst
men—which has already been mentioned in the preceding section in relation to 3:5. This readily relates the
water theme with the second basic theme of this scene:
God as Spirit (4:23, 24). It is quite anachronistic to
think that Jesus (or the evangelist) is advocating 'inward'
worship over against communal and ritualist forms. The
contrast is of the same kind as those which we have
already seen, and indeed takes them up and carries them
further; what is being talked about is precisely a worship
which is led by Jesus into the presence of the Father—
as he said to Nicodemus, 'from above' rather than 'from
below'. The new order, which is again being referred to
here, is one in which heaven and earth are brought together 'in the Spirit', not held apart from one another, as
'on earth'. The temple is not to be annihilated and
'spiritualised' inwardly, but is to be located bodily in
Jesus himself (cf 2:21).

Once again the question whether there is any reference
to the sacraments must be raised here. As in the earlier
passage centred on Nicodemus there is nothing explicit
in the actual presentation to suggest that baptism is being
talked about. Indeed one might say that the imagery is in
fact contrary to this because it is water being drunk that is
being talked about (4:14). It is, however, using far too
narrow a concept of baptism to associate it solely with
being washed by water. Consider, for instance, 'For by

one Spirit we were all baptised into one body—Jews or
Greeks, slaves or free—and all were made to *drink* of one
Spirit' (1 Cor 12:13), and one of the early christian
symbols of baptism is that of the hart drinking from the
flowing stream (Ps 42). The connection between water
and the Spirit, which is explicitly developed here, is
however a factor which would, most likely, have drawn
attention to the baptismal significance of the whole
passage, and the way in which this chapter stands as a
second commentary on the earlier incidents, paralleling
the Nicodemus discourse, makes this connection, at a
secondary level of interpretation and development, not
at all unreasonable or unlikely.

The second scene of this incident involves the disciples
and Jesus in discourse (4:27–38). There is considerable
parallelism with the previous scene indicating the same
differences in depth of perspective (the disciples are
involved in a misunderstanding over food—4:31, 32—
as the woman was over water). The true food of Jesus is
to do the will of his Father (4:34) and this is to draw all
men to himself. The whole passage is about the developing faith of the christian community over against that of
the individual—the Samaritan woman. This theme is
carried on into the harvest imagery in which the reaper
(primarily Jesus) is already at work. Here we have a
clear example of the gospel's understanding of the
eschatological age as already come about, 'realised'.

The discourse ends with a somewhat puzzling proverb,
and its application, concerning those who have sown and
those who will reap. There are a host of interpretations
here depending upon whether one sees this saying as coming from Jesus himself or reflecting the later apostolic
evangelisation of Samaria and the problems that such
activity produced as the result of rival factions at work

(cf 1 Cor 3:8). What seems most likely, however, is that the relative confusion to be found here in Jesus' mono-logue (4:34–38) reflects the, not unhealthy, confusion in the mind of the church concerning the future or real-ised eschatology which her existence, through the presence of the spirit, embodied or prefigured. It is a mistake to think that in the fourth gospel there is a concept of the 'last days' only as now realised.

This brings to an end the set of signs, incidents and commentaries with which the presentation of Jesus' 'public ministry' opens. If its overall import can be summed up in a single phrase it is probably 'the new beginning' in which the old order is seen as being trans-formed into something new—something much richer and with deeper dimensions; and the way in which this comes about can be summarised by the closing words of this section: 'For we have heard for ourselves, and we know that this is really the Saviour of the world' (4:42).

1. When we worship God in church are we closer to temple worship or worship 'in the spirit'? Is there any danger of our confusing these two and thus betraying Christ's mission?

2. Does our liturgical worship express the relationship between physical, tangible actuality and the living message in the same way as John's literary and dramatic style does? Should it? Could it? What value does it have if it does not?

Jn 4:43–5:47. The life-giving word

Here we have two miracles of healing followed by a discourse of remarkable quality. It is well worthwhile taking a look at a version which lays out the poetical and declamatory parts in poetical form. The effect is to bring out the relation of 'narrative' to discourse in a heightened way, especially in this section—as also in chapters 3, 6, 8 and 10.

There is some difficulty with regard to 'placing' the first incident of healing (4:46–54) in relation to what has gone before and what is to come. From some points of view it can be regarded as the conclusion to the preceding section—it is concerned, as that is, with the development of faith from one level to another. Also at the beginning of chapter 5 Jesus leaves Galilee and goes up to Jerusalem again, as if starting a new chapter. Nevertheless if one compares these two miracles with the two episodes of chapter 2 one notices a marked similarity. In each case the first takes place at Cana (2:1; 4:46) and then the scene changes to Jerusalem (2:13; 5:1); and in each case the discourse which follows embraces both of the incidents. We can conclude, then, that although this first section is basically pivotal, nevertheless since comment on it is to be found only after the following miracle, from the point of view of the presentation of its significance it forms a unit together with the whole of chapter 5—two healing miracles and a discourse.

There is a point worth noticing in the introductory 'stage-setting' verses (4:43–45). There seems to be a total lack of logic in the redactor's comment (4:44) about a prophet having no honour in his own land; for Jesus is leaving Judaea, which is not his country, and going to Galilee where the Galileans welcome him with apparent faith (4:45). The point however is that, from the theological point of view of the redactor, the superficial faith of the Galileans (to be demonstrated both immediately and later) is basically no better than the disbelief of 'the Jews'.

In the story which follows of the healing of the royal

official's son (4:46–54) we are forced at once to compare it with the synoptic account of the healing of the centurion's boy (Mt 8:5–13; Lk 7:1–10). There are minor distinctive differences but such a welter of similarities as to make it highly probable that one single incident is at the root of these two different accounts. Which account represents the more accurate tradition it is impossible to say.

An interesting feature which backs up the parallelism between this whole section and the previous one (2:1–4: 42), which has already been mentioned, is the similarity of certain features in this account to those in the wedding feast at Cana: Jesus has just returned to Galilee, to the same place; someone comes to him with a request; Jesus seems at first sight to refuse it, but on the supplicant persisting grants their request; this leads other people to believe in him; and then Jesus departs to Jerusalem and the temple, the incident finishing without any discourse. It may well be that the original material has been edited to produce this effect.

A point where editing is quite clear is 4:48–49, where Jesus is reported as saying 'Unless you see signs and wonders you will not believe . . .' There is no parallel to this in the synoptic accounts, and the verses read like an insertion. In some ways the comment is uncharacteristic of Jesus' concern for the sick (though see Mk 7:24–30), and in the context it even seems rather unfair. We have here an editorial addition (of what period it is impossible to say, though certainly not belonging to the final redaction) the whole purpose of which is to alter the significance of the incident—at least for the moment. The result of the insertion is to throw the emphasis from the actual healing to the inadequacies of initial belief and an attitude which demands miraculous wonders. We are then shown the progression from that to a belief in Jesus based on what he fundamentally stands for and represents, namely life (which of course returns us in a circle to the healing motif, and thus on to the next sign).

Modern archaeological discoveries have proved the accuracy of the details of this story about the cripple at the pool of Bethzatha (5:1–15). We should also notice what a detailed character portrait is presented of this rather stupid and fumbling man who even ends up, apparently without malice, in betraying his benefactor to his enemies (5:15–16). The point of this whole incident is to bring into sharp contrast and connection the healing and life-giving work of Jesus and the laws of sabbath observance as interpreted by the pharisees; and the discourse which follows starts off precisely by concentrating on this point.

This discourse falls into two parts, the first of which (5:16–30) starts with a dialogue in which Jesus defends his healing people on the sabbath with the claim that he is doing his Father's work (5:16–18). It is important to realise that this must be seen in a particular context. In the old testament we are told how God rested from his work on the sabbath, thus making this day holy and one to be observed (Ex 20:11). It was soon realised, however, that this could not be taken simply at its face value; God must continue to work on the sabbath, otherwise everything would fall into nothingness, and anyway he can be seen at work since people are born and die even on the sabbath. Rabbinic teaching indicates that the activity of God on the sabbath was seen to be precisely life-giving; and Jesus' claim to work on behalf of his Father on the sabbath must have been seen as a claim to share the life-giving work of the Father (cf especially 5:21).

Whether this claim was made by Jesus himself or by the evangelist on his behalf is a difficult question to answer; but by comparison with accounts of 'sabbath-breaking' in the synoptics it looks as if the tradition, if not the full theological explicitation, goes right back to Jesus and his confrontation with the religious authorities. The theological implications are further spelled out in the speech that follows, though the whole of it has so many characteristics of the specifically Jewish style of argument, and contains references to current Jewish practices (eg with regard to the father/son and master/ apprentice relationships), that one should be wary of regarding it as merely a later christian theological development.

The speech starts (5:19–25) by stating the relationship of the Son to the Father with considerable clarity. Their work is one, yet it all comes to the Son through the Father. Life is given and judgment (the establishment of a just order) is made, and all this is brought to reality through men listening to the word of God and believing it (both the miracles are accomplished purely with Jesus' word). Apart from this the emphasis of these verses is on the fact that the Father, through his Son, is now working amongst men in a more intensive way than ever before: heaven and earth are truly joined in Jesus' relation to his Father and in the work which they do together. In other words the messianic or eschatological age has come amongst us.

The rest of the verses (5:26–30) of this first part of the discourse contain an interestingly different emphasis. This is all the more significant since they can be seen to form a parallel version of what has just gone before; they might well be based on some original common source, but would have developed separately and differently

within the Johannine tradition and would have been
added at some stage in the later editing of the original
gospel. The emphasis here is on a future rather than a
realised eschatology. The balance is being redressed by
their inclusion, and the ambiguity, which we have
already drawn attention to, is being re-established. Apart
from this the theme is the same as before: Jesus shares the
life-giving work of the Father, and this is transmitted
through his life-giving word (5:28).

The second part of the discourse (5:31–47) has the
structure of a trial. It would seem to presuppose someone
saying 'You only bear witness to yourself, and such witness is invalid'. Jesus accepts the point but insists that he
has other witnesses (5:31, 32). In the verses that follow
they are listed, strophe by strophe: first there is John the
Baptist (5:33–35); but even more powerful than this as
testimony are the very works which Jesus performs
(5:36); these come from the Father, who himself
witnesses to Jesus, though 'the Jews' cannot appreciate
this because the law which he has given (understood as
both external and interior) is no longer a living reality in
them (5:37, 38); and finally if they look at the scriptures
they will see that they too witness to whom Jesus is
(5:39, 40). This latter is a theme developed at length in
the synoptics; we have remarked earlier that in John
it is not made so explicit, nevertheless it is a major
feature of the theology of this gospel.

The last section (5:41–47) indicates the outcome of the
'trial'. Jesus is condemned because they cannot accept
such witness. The reason for this is that they seek after
their own glory rather than God's (5:44). The passage
ends with the condemnation being turned back on the
judges themselves; and because the old law (Moses)
witnesses to Jesus, the old law now itself condemns those

who claim to rely on it. Here we have a reasonably clear expression of the way in which in John's thought the presence of Jesus himself is what makes man, in his reaction to him, choose life and light or turn away from him into darkness. The dualism in John is forced on man himself by his own reaction to what is offered.

1. Would it make any difference to John's message in this section if one saw the 'miracles' as psychological effects of encounter with a very remarkable personality rather than as a manifestation of divine power?

2. Is the real point of Jesus' appeal to 'witness' to justify his claims, or is it to force people into a position where they have to be either for or against him?

Jn 6:1–71. The bread of life

Chapter 6 has often been regarded as being out of place, and many attempts have been made to rearrange sections of the gospel in order to make it cohere chronologically and geographically. The usual result is to destroy the overall theological consistency and development; and quite apart from this, such attempts are based on a fundamentally wrong approach to this gospel. Although it is now seen to be more radically based on authentic traditional material than was once believed to be possible, it is nevertheless quite uninterested in chronology for its own sake, though overall it follows a time sequence similar to that of the synoptics; this time sequence, it should be noted however, is itself of theological significance, lesser time patterns for the most part are not.

Although there is an overall lack of interest in chronological and geographical 'accuracy' throughout Christ's ministry, and as a result some shifting around of incidents for theological purposes, nevertheless within particular incidents there is often a considerable effort put into presenting the material as a dramatic whole. Chapter 6 is a good example of this, and although the interrelation of traditional incidents (eg those of the multiplication of loaves and walking on the sea, cf Mt 14:13–33; Mk 6:30–52) may well have affected aspects of the structure, nevertheless the whole episode has been shaped with considerable ingenuity. This process is not, however, without visibility and in places the shaping, with material not totally suitable, can easily be seen.

The overall structure consists first of all of an account of two signs (or miracles), with a note on the way in which people tried to seize Jesus and make him king inserted between them; this is then followed (with deliberate continuity) by a lengthy and magnificent discourse on the 'bread of life' which looks back directly to the multiplication of loaves. The conclusion depicts the reaction to this discourse and leaves Jesus alone with his disciples who proclaim their belief in him in terms of true messianic fulfilment, which is the implication of the whole story and discourse.

(i) Jn 6:1–21. Multiplication of loaves and walking on the water

The multiplication of loaves is the only miracle of Jesus' public ministry which is reported in all four gospels. Thus it immediately raises the whole question of the authenticity of Johannine tradition in relation to that of the synoptics. Many people have tried to demonstrate that John is copying the synoptics and not any independent tradition of his own. But if this were so it would be necessary to show the reasons for the differences which do occur between the accounts, and this has never satisfactorily been done.

The whole issue is considerably complicated by the fact that in Mark and Matthew there are two multiplication miracles recounted which are almost certainly different presentations of one actual incident. We cannot go into the issues involved here, but they are presented in detail for example in R. E. Brown, *The Gospel according to John* pp 236–244. His conclusion is that whilst the Johannine account is not copied from any one of the synoptics, nor pieced together from several of them, and thus represents a basically independent account, nevertheless an occasional detail has probably been added from Mark by the final redactor.

Several interesting points arise out of John's account of this incident. First we should note the reference to its taking place about passover time. This may be for the sake of emphasising the eucharistic implications which are to be spelt out in the discourse, but it is interesting to note that, without any emphasis on this point, there are hints at this dating in the synoptic accounts as well. It would not seem, then, that this reference can be regarded as purely an editorial insertion.

Another point of interest is that there is considerable eucharistic reference in the actual account of the miracle here (cf particularly 6:11), just as there is also in the synoptic accounts. Considering that this theme is so thoroughly written up in the later part of the chapter it is somewhat surprising to find it actually penetrating the miracle account itself. One must conclude that the eucharistic symbolism had begun to affect this tradition before it ever received the theological development given to it by the discourse.

In all this speculation one should not lose sight of the very evident messianic symbolism in this incident. The feeding of a large multitude in the desert is a clear symbol of the presence of God in his final intervention. In fact here in John we are told that its immediate result was that the people tried to seize Jesus and make him king. They had got half the point, but the whole way in which the chapter develops indicates that this, like earlier incidents which we have seen, is an example of a faith which is too shallow. Its immediate result is to separate Jesus from his fellow-men and his disciples and thus to open the way for the description of the crossing of the lake in the rising storm which follows.

It seems odd in a way that this scene on the lake (6: 16–21) is inserted between the multiplication of loaves and the discourse on the bread of life, for the latter seems to refer back only to the former. If the author of the gospel were simply a creative artist building up a theological picture it would be hard to explain, but as we have seen he was concerned, more than passingly, with tradition. It would seem (and comparison with Mark and Matthew confirm this) that these two incidents are closely bound together in primitive tradition and are regarded as inseparable.

The possible reasons for this are a matter of speculation, but one in particular is worth noting. We have already remarked on the specific reference to this taking place at passover time (6:4) and seen how this helps weld the discourse to the sign which it comments upon. For this reason the passover significance of the walking on the water must be more than casual. The passover and exodus are closely connected together in the old testament tradition; and Ps 77, poetically describing the exodus, says: 'Your way was on the sea, your path on

the many waters; yet your footsteps were not seen.' The
subject here is, of course, God, and this leads to the most
interesting aspect of this story in John.

The difference between the synoptic and Johannine
accounts are considerable with regard to detail, but the
most important point is their overall emphasis. In the
synoptics the miracle is primarily presented as a manifestation of divine power (though there are other interesting elements in Matthew); in John the whole emphasis has been thrown on to Jesus' revelation of his
identity: 'It is I' (6:20). This is to be understood on two
levels, and there can be little doubt that the second is a
declaration of the divine name 'I am'—this, John is
telling us, is who Jesus really is. There can now be seen
to be a further connection between these two miraculous
happenings and the discourse. The pattern of this latter,
as we are about to see, is basically that of a movement
away from a wrong understanding of the life and
nourishment which God gives to man to a final declaration of faith in him when Jesus has been left alone
with his disciples. This closely reflects the movement here
in the miracle stories from the wrong appreciation of
Jesus as messiah to the declaration of his identity in the
boat.

*1. Do you think the figures and details given with regard to the
multiplication miracle are meant to be understood symbolically
or factually, ie as indicative of a tradition arising from eye-
witness accounts? In which would you see most value?*

*2. Is there any analogy between the way in which the people's
reaction to the multiplication of loaves was to try and make Jesus
king—the wrong sort of king—and the traditional forms in
which the church tries to honour and use the 'blessed sacrament'
as God's presence amongst men?*

(ii) Jn 6:25–71. The bread of life

The first ten verses (6:25–34) form an introduction to
the main body of the discourse. They contain a number of
problems and awkward interrelations which indicate the
editing which has gone on to build up the overall
dramatic structure; but the theological development is
clear and without hesitation. We start with the now
familiar pattern of inadequate belief being led on to
something greater, and this is done through the transference of the subject from one level to another (6:25–
27). The people's response to this is 'what shall we do?'
and Jesus' answer is 'have faith' (6:28–29). We know
of the controversy between the 'followers' of Paul and of
James over 'faith or works'. Here we have in effect the
Johannine solution: the work that must be done is
precisely God's work, and this is to believe in him whom
God has sent. This only makes sense, and then it makes
profound sense, on the Johannine understanding of the
gospel that there is no separation of body and spirit,
material and idea, earth and heaven, but these are firmly
held together in Jesus and his relation to the Father. To
believe in him is to receive him (1:12), to live with him,
and to act in his name, and thus experience through him
the presence and love of the Father. This is partly to
anticipate, but it gives a clue, I suggest, to the way in
which faith and works, for John, are one reality.

The result of this assertion is to make the people
suspicious of Jesus and they demand proof. The sign they
ask for is precisely an eschatological sign (6:30, 31), and
Jesus' answer is to the effect that the times to which they
look forward are here and now present (6:32, 33). This
has been expressed in terms of manna and bread, and so
this now leads straight into the discourse on the bread of
life proper. The whole of the discourse can be seen as an

explanation and development of Jesus' answer. Before going on to this, however, it is worth noting the considerable similarity in style of this introductory passage to the dialogue between Jesus and Nicodemus (3:1–21).

The first main section of the discourse (6:35–50) is built up in a way which is typical of the Jewish homiletic technique at the time of Christ, and it is within the bounds of possibility that it represents, or part represents, a discourse which Jesus himself gave in a synagogue, as is asserted in 6:59. It seems more likely, however, that it is a construct of elements which might well have gone back to very primitive sources. One should note the way in which the passage concludes (in a manner characteristic of such homiletic structures) with an inclusive return to its beginning (6:48–50 and 6:35).

Although one cannot use this to back up any theory of its origin it is significant that the whole section is based on themes of fulfilment from the old testament which could have been understood (particularly in a passover context) by people who were completely ignorant of later christian theological development. These themes are primarily sapiential, though dependent upon messianic themes: the image of the banquet is traditionally messianic and is noticeably used in this sense in the synoptics; and we have already pointed out how the miracle of multiplication was understood messianically.

The discourse is concerned, however, to transfer this understanding on to another plane, and it has partial precedent for this in the transformation of the idea of the messianic banquet which is to be found in the wisdom literature. Here human food, whether of earthly or divine origin, is replaced by the word, or wisdom, of God. This transformation is to be found in Isaiah (55:1–11) and in Amos (8:11–13) and is developed in

Sirach (eg 15:3) and Proverbs (9:5); references to some
of these passages seem to occur in the discourse, and in
6:45 there is a direct quotation of Is 54:13. This whole
theme fits in well with the summary statement of the
gospel to be found in the prologue.

There is also, however, undeniable sacramental
symbolism present in this first part of the discourse, as
there was in the account of the feeding of the multitude;
it is nevertheless clearly secondary. An example is the
way in which Jesus identifies himself here with the bread
of life (6:35) whereas in chapter 4 there is no identification with the similar concept of living water.

The opening verse (6:35) insists that true life, true
food, true drink are in effect all one reality, and that
reality is Christ himself. The next verses (6:36–40)
spell out the necessity of believing in Jesus and accepting
the Father as the source of all he does if one is to receive
this life. (These verses have a structure which seems to
indicate that they have a previous history and come from
a tradition earlier than the actual formation of this
discourse.) Jesus' speech is then broken into by 'the
Jews' who start to 'murmur' (6:41, 43) in a way reminiscent of the Israelites against Moses in the desert. In his
answer (6:44–47) to their question 'How does he say, "I
have come down from heaven"?' (6:42) Jesus simply
points out that he is from God and is sent by God. If the
Jews replace disbelief with belief they will be brought to
the Father by Jesus himself who will give them the life
which he shares with the Father. The passage ends by
returning once again to its beginning and asserting the
difference between the two levels of reality which Jesus
has come to transpose (6:48–50).

What follows now (6:51–59) is in fact a repetition of
this very discourse; it has however undergone a radical

transformation. The bread of life has now become the eucharistic bread; what has only been hinted at in all that has gone before is now explicitly stated.

There is so much parallelism of content and structure between this section of the discourse (6:51–59) and the preceding section (6:35–50—which we have seen to be complete in itself anyway) as to make it look as if it had either been constructed out of other material to match or else was based on the same tradition yet developed with very significant changes. These changes representing other material are connected with the eucharistic institution and liturgy, eg 'Truly, truly, I say to you, unless you eat the flesh of the Son of man and drink his blood, you have no life in you' (6:53, 54) and 'The bread which I shall give for the life of the world is my flesh' (6:51). Compare these with the synoptic and Pauline descriptions of the 'institution' (Mk 14:22–25; Mt 26:26–29; Lk 22:15–20; 1 Cor 11:23–25).

The question which arises is when and how did this second part of the discourse get added to the first? was it early or late? was it to make explicit what was already there or to contradict with a different attitude the outlook of the original gospel? This last question can most easily be answered. The clear, if unemphasised and only secondary, eucharistic references to be found throughout the whole of this chapter up to now would indicate a change of emphasis rather than a radical change of outlook. The style would seem not to be that of the final redactor but of an intermediate editor, and would thus suggest a middle position in the development of the gospel.

It has been suggested with considerable plausibility (R. E. Brown, *op cit* pp 287–299) that the material used for this part of the discourse has been taken originally from chapter 13, and in fact represents the Johannine version of the 'institution' which is so strangely absent from there. There is, it has been pointed out, a gap at precisely the point where this material would most conveniently fit in and an interesting reference there to 'eating my bread' (13:18). The theological perspectives of the fourth gospel (rather than any narrow biographical interest) would have made this move completely reasonable. Its absence from the 'account' of what went on at the last supper would hardly have worried the christian community within which we have envisaged the gospel as developing; and its presence in chapter 6 would have been obvious to them.

It remains for a few particular comments to be made on this section of the discourse. 6:52 is parallel to 6:41, 42 in the earlier part of the discourse; both involve misunderstanding and puzzlement on the part of Jesus' hearers. In neither case does Jesus give a straight answer to their questions; in fact here (6:53, 54) he compounds the difficulty which would be experienced by anyone who did not understand this sacramentally. It is interesting to note that not only does the fourth gospel resist any temptation to overspiritualise the humanity of Jesus but it equally resists overspiritualisation of the reality of the eucharistic flesh and blood. The word 'flesh' used here probably represents the Aramaic original in a way in which the other traditions, with their use of 'body' (for which there is no real Aramaic equivalent) do not. Characteristically, in its intense spirituality this gospel is completely down to earth.

Comparison of 6:54 with 6:53 indicates the way in which eternal life is the result of being in close communion with Jesus. This communion is a reflection of the communion between the Son and the Father and the life which is bestowed flows from this. This whole passage is full of the Johannine concept of realised eschatology (the idea that the final time of God's intervention has arrived), but once again we see indications of a future eschatology as well: 'He ... has eternal life, and I will raise him up at the last day' (6:54). The eschatology of John can best be described as 'inaugurated'.

The final verses of the chapter (6:60–71) are continuous not so much with the explicitly eucharistic part of the discourse as with the previous sections. The remark about the flesh being of no avail, only the spirit giving life (6:63) refers back beyond the eucharistic section and is in fact taking up the distinction between flesh and spirit which we saw in looking at chapter 4. Another theme which we have already seen and which now comes up again is the way in which full confrontation with Jesus divides men for and against him; the 'Jesus-situation' is the situation in which men bring judgment upon themselves. The reaction of the disciples (6:66) who will not accept Jesus is similar to that of the fools who will not accept the presence of personified wisdom amongst men and who will not come to his banquet (Sir 24:19–20); again Jesus is being portrayed as the wisdom of God amongst men.

In the faith expressed by the twelve (6:67–70) we seem to have a Johannine parallel to the synoptic account of the scene at Caesarea Philippi where Peter in particular proclaims his faith in Jesus (Mk 8:27; Mt 16:13); but remember that we have already had, in the introductory first chapter, what seems like a partial presentation of this scene—geographical and chronological exactitude with regard to this sort of thing are of little interest to the author. The reference to betrayal by Judas (6:70, 71) indicates that even within the circle

closest to Jesus the self-judgment (just referred to) due
to his impact continues to operate.

*Does the 'bread of life' theme help us to see how accepting the
word of God in Christ is not a matter of intellectual assent but of
sharing in the life which is being given? Is this made obvious by
the eucharistic liturgy? Should this be the main function, or a
peripheral aspect, of the eucharist?*

Jn 7:1–8:59. The feast of tabernacles

These two chapters (7, 8) which deal with Jesus' presence
in Jerusalem at the feast of tabernacles have a difficult,
and at first sight puzzling, structure. They are extremely
composite, made up of all sorts of snatches of material.
In the second part we can detect at least three separate
discourses, but anyway that chapter (8) is consistently
made up of discourse material; in the first part (7) we
have a number of discourse snippets worked in with
narrative material. There are no miracles in the whole
section, but it becomes clear on examination that this
first section does in fact represent the sign which the
discourses which follow then comment upon.

The sign in this case is somewhat different from those
with which we have up to now been concerned, with the
exception of the cleansing of the temple incident (2:13–
22) which is in several ways similar. Both that incident
and the present one, which is even more composite
than that was, take place in the temple, and both are
precisely confrontations between Jesus, with his claims,
and the authorities and the people. The confrontation in
this case takes place more at the level of ideas, and this is
why there is a considerable quantity of 'discourse
material' interwoven with it. But it is this confrontation,

in which Jesus argues, is called on to declare himself, is
denounced, nearly arrested, and so on, that constitutes
the significant action (ie the sign) to which the discourses of the following chapter refer back and reflect
upon. After the great crescendoing discourses of the preceding chapters this collection of various pieces—which
nevertheless have an overall coherence and contain some
of the profoundest themes—comes as a welcome relaxation.

(i) Jn 7:1–52. Jesus at the feast

The first few verses (7:1–13) set the theme. Jesus'
brethren, who do not believe in him, nevertheless
recognise him as a man of public significance and,
puzzled by him, urge him to stop prevaricating and
declare himself. It is interesting to note that in John
miraculous power does not, as it does in the synoptics,
produce belief; Jesus' brethren have seen his power and
yet do not believe. It is the deed combined with the word,
in all the depth of the significance of both of these, that
reveal God's presence in Jesus to those who do not turn
away from the encounter.

The way in which Jesus refuses to come to the feast
(7:8) and yet comes (7:10) is not a contradiction but a
straightforward example of Johannine double meaning.
The feast of tabernacles had a specifically messianic
connotation; the implication is that Jesus is not coming
to fulfil the people's expectation in the way they think,
but in a quite different way: he is both not coming to the
feast and coming to it. Here we have the usual transference of the meaning of the situation from one level to
another.

In parentheses it can be added that this scene brings
to an end a sequence of incidents where comparison

between John and the synoptics reveals something very interesting. In 6:15, as we have seen, the people try to make Jesus king; in 6:31 they ask for miraculous bread; here in 7:3 his brethren want Jesus to go to Jerusalem to show his power. Compare these with the synoptic account of the temptations in the desert. Is this latter a dramatic presentation of the temptations Jesus encountered in his ministry? Are the characteristic roles of John and the synoptics in this instance reversed?

The main body of the confrontation is made up of two passages, 7:14–36 and 37–52; there are in fact a number of parallels between them and it is possible that in effect we have the same original material developed in different ways. The whole scene has strong dramatic structure with its entries and exits, with Jesus holding the front of the stage arguing with the authorities and the crowd, whilst back stage they are plotting his destruction.

Jesus is effectively accused (7:15) of being a false teacher because he has not had the traditional (scribal) instruction. He retorts that his doctrine is from God; the scribes claim Moses as their teacher but in having betrayed Moses it is they themselves who are out of order. This is a theme to be found readily in the other gospels. It introduces once again the sabbath-breaking theme (7:21) and there is a direct reference back to 5:2–9. Jesus' answer this time, by introducing circumcision and the mosaic law, is in effect a claim that what he has to give is life to the whole man rather than a part of him, and that his works are precisely the accomplishment of what the law itself really stands for.

We are now shown (7:25–31) the confusion, doubt and expectation which Jesus' presence produces. Jesus' comments point the irony of the way in which people know, and yet do not know, where he is from. This leads to a declaration which refers to his coming death and glorification and the need for a true faith in order to be with him (cf 13:33; 14:19), and which at the same time must have indicated, to the church, the way in which the word of God has indeed gone 'among the Greeks to teach the Greeks' (7:36).

One should notice how rich this whole section is with the motif of divine wisdom incarnate among men. Bar 3:14–15 mentions the way in which men do not know where wisdom is from. Job 28:12 raises the same subject. In Wis 9:10 and Sir 24:8 wisdom is sent by God in the same way as Jesus claims to be (7:16). And finally Jesus' words at the end (7:34) are very similar to those of wisdom in Prov 1:28–29. The incarnate wisdom theme applied to Jesus is one of increasing intensity.

The feast of tabernacles was of extreme importance, being associated with the dedication of the temple (1 Kg 8:2) and later with the coming 'day of the Lord'. In Zechariah it is given explicit messianic content and associated with the outpouring of the Spirit, when the 'living waters' will flow out of Jerusalem over all the land (Zech 14:8). This is the background of Jesus' climactic appearance (7:37). On the seventh day (7:37), when all the most significant ritual was repeated seven times. Jesus declares:

> If anyone thirst
> let him who believes in me
> come to me and drink.
> As the scripture has said,
> 'Out of his heart shall flow rivers
>   of living water' (7:37, 38)

It is not possible to identify the scriptural quotation (it may be from a commentary or from an Aramaic translation), and thus the exact reference is indeterminable; but the context would seem to indicate the scriptures especially connected with the feast of tabernacles. The Greek of the whole passage is also ambiguous and some authorities have made the quotation refer to the believer rather than to Jesus (cf the RSV, which differs from the above). But the context favours the reading and interpretation given above.

It may be, however, that the reference is to Moses' miracle in the desert producing water from the rock. The evangelist probably accepts a multiple understanding for we see the people arguing whether 'this man' is the messiah or the prophet (like Moses—see commentary on 1:21). (Incidentally the last words of the chapter (7:52) should read: 'Search and you will see that the prophet will not rise from Galilee', not as in the RSV.) There is obviously an extreme richness of ideas in the way in which, in this particular context, Jesus declares himself to be the source of life and of the spirit. We have already seen him manifesting himself as the source of 'living water' (Jn 4), and his body as replacing the temple (Jn 2). Here in effect these themes are welded together and given a further significance.

1. Now that Christ, who is himself incarnate wisdom, has come amongst us, do we know how and where he is to be found? or does the same situation portrayed in this chapter still in some way pertain?

2. Has the answer to the question who exactly Jesus is been definitively given to us, or are we still looking for it?

(ii) **Jn 8:12–59. The testimony of Jesus**
[The first eleven verses of chapter 8 about the woman

taken in adultery do not belong to John, and are missing
in all the earliest manuscripts. The style would seem to
indicate that it is a misplaced fragment from the synoptic
tradition. Although it contains a number of important
lessons for us it would be out of place to discuss it here,
for it would spoil the flow of the Johannine argument.]

There are three separate discourses here, which have
nevertheless been put together as a whole. The first
(8:12–20) has obviously had a long history of literary
manipulation and build-up. In many ways it refers back
to the earlier part of chapter 7, yet there are cross-
references in all directions. It starts with Jesus being
presented as the light of the world. This is a theme very
much connected with the messianism of the feast of
tabernacles. Zechariah, whose theology as we have
already seen is dominant with regard to the feast, talks
about continuous day, and light even in the evening
(14:8). Another image, coming from Exodus and possibly connected in the evangelist's mind with the water
from the rock (Exodus provides a continuous theme
throughout John), is that of the pillar of fire (Ex 13:21).
The likelihood of its presence here is increased by the
way in which it was later transformed to apply to wisdom
as the 'imperishable light of the law' (Wis 18:3–4).

From here the discourse moves on once more to the
theme of witness and judgment. The greater part of this is
parallel to similar material in chapter 5. If we can sum
up its significance it is as follows: the criticism which is
throughout being brought to bear on Jesus is turned by
him, with the backing of tradition, on to his accusers. It is
their own principles that condemn them, and which justify the claims being made by (or for) Jesus.

The next subsectional discourse (8:21–30) moves
continuously back and forward in the context of mis-

understanding. In all their comments and their puzzlement the Jews are ironically stating a truth about Jesus
which they do not understand. Everything that he says
indicates a different plane of reality—the spiritual—from
that with which they are concerned. This difference will
in effect only be brought out clearly when Jesus has been
raised up. This, of course, refers to the crucifixion, but
implicit in this is the raising up by the Father; these together manifest to men the true nature of Jesus as Christ.
Twice here the discourse involves the name 'I am' by
which Jesus associates himself with the Father.

The third and longest discourse (8:31–59) develops
this theme further. The Jews play into Jesus' hands
by invoking their descent from Abraham. They think,
however, only of the privileges that this brings, completely forgetting the obligations. The dialogue, as a
result, spells out fully the differences between true and
false fidelity to one's traditions. The train of thought in
this way introduced leads to the final and climactic
declaration that 'before Abraham was, I am' (8:58). The
Jews, on the basis of their myopic and stunted presuppositions (which form the basis of their being condemned as devil's brood (8:44)), correctly want to stone
Jesus for such blasphemy.

Before commenting on the nature and historicity of
this claim we want to note the way in which the 'I am' at
the end reflects back on, and forms a (partial) inclusion
with, the 'I am' at the beginning of the whole discourse
(8:12). This latter is not an absolute use of the term but is
predicated with 'the light of the world'; thus it carries no
claim to divinity. It is however precisely because of the
full implications of what Jesus is, in other words the full
content of that predicate, that it can be said of him that
he is, absolutely. As in all the discourses this content is

largely, if far from totally, expressed and indicated in the complex discourse which follows; the inclusion gives it a coherence beyond its literary form.

Is it possible that such a claim to divinity as presented in this discourse could actually have been made by Jesus, or is the scene fundamentally a construct of the evangelist? Certainly it is this latter, but does that necessarily preclude the former? In any simple way I suggest that it probably does preclude it; but nevertheless, bearing in mind the whole character of the gospel which should have become clear to us by now, it is near inconceivable that such a scene should be totally without some sort of traditional origin. There is witness to a similar claim in the synoptics (Mk 14:62), though this might be equally 'theological'—an interpretation built up in dramatic form. More than this cannot be said.

With regard to the whole question of actual historical 'accuracy' here one should bear in mind that, perhaps more than any other section of the gospel, these two chapters (7 & 8) represent the early struggle and cross-accusations between the church and judaism, and they must be read in this light. They express more than anything else the awareness of the church of what Jesus means and how he relates to the judaic tradition from which he springs. At the same time, however, these chapters sum up, and present in literary/dramatic form, the struggle which took place throughout Jesus' public ministry. They present this actual struggle together with its ultimate implications: and perhaps for this reason its central placing in the book of signs is something more than a mere literary artifice.

When Jesus said 'Before Abraham was, I am' (8 : 58) the Jews took up stones to kill him because they regarded it as blasphemous. If we believe, we do not regard it as blasphemy but as truth; but are we able to think of Jesus—the person who is talking—as being before Abraham was, whilst at the same time appreciating him as really a human being? Is the traditional solution of 'two natures in one person' effectively faithful to the mind of the fourth evangelist? and does this formula help or hinder us today in receiving and handing on the whole of Christ without distortion?

Jn 9:1–10:39. Judgment by the light

(i) Jn 9:1–41. The man born blind

Chapter 9 contains the sign which is going to receive its 'commentary' in the discourses of chapter 10. At first sight it might seem that chapter 9 is complete in itself, containing the sign—the miracle of curing the man born blind (9:1–7)—and the comment upon it to be found in the dramatic dialogue between the man and the Jews and Jesus which follows. If this were really so, however, it would be a startling example of a simplicity quite uncharacteristic of John. We have seen again and again how complex the concept of sign is; it is not the miraculous or significant happening as such so much as this together with its associations and immediate significance —consider how the two incidents of the wedding feast at Cana and the cleansing of the temple (Jn 2) form the overall 'sign' which is reflected upon in the following discourses, or the multiplication of loaves and the walking on the water (Jn 6) in relation to the bread of life discourse; or again, more interestingly still, the way in which the complex encounter during the feast of tabernacles (Jn 7) formed the 'sign' to which the later discourses (Jn 8) referred back. Here it is the whole of the encounter between the man and the Jews together with

Jesus' overall action, presence and significance that constitutes the 'sign' in its fullness.

The scene depicted is probably the most dramatically powerful in the gospel, but it has depths which go well beyond the drama. It opens with a problem (9:1, 2) and a monologue by Jesus (9:3–5) which helps to tie it in with the development of ideas in the gospel as a whole. Then comes the actual miracle of healing, described with great economy (9:6, 7); there are all the signs of a primitive source being used here, but (as so often) there are also theological (especially, though not exclusively, sacramental) motifs present even here.

After this (9:8–41) we have what amounts to a straight-forward trial scene in which of course the real defendant is Jesus himself, with the man-born-blind as his effective advocate. The trial ends in the rejection of Jesus and his followers by the Jews; but this 'judgment' is in effect turned by Jesus on the Jews themselves to their condemnation (9:39–41).

What should be noted is that as the condemnation of Jesus by the Jewish authorities progresses, the understanding of Jesus by the man increases from near ignorance, 'The man called Jesus' (9:11), through 'He is a prophet' (9:17) and 'If he were not from God' (9:33), to the climactic acceptance of Jesus as 'the Son of Man' (9:35, 38). The construction we see here is clearly the work of the evangelist, it has all the marks throughout of a carefully built-up apologetic confrontation between christians and Jews. Apart from the details of the miracle and some of the associations of the first few verses it is impossible to attribute simple historicity to this scene. One should note in particular the way in which the inserted comment of the redactor (9:22, 23) reflects the late situation in which, at the culminating height of this controversy, Jews who believed in Christ were being ejected from the synagogue.

In this context a number of apparent problems about the dialogue become clear. For instance, if this were a reported incident the phrase about the Son of Man in the conversation between Jesus and the man born blind would be puzzling; in the context of an apologetical (and/or catechetical) dialogue the problem vanishes—it clinches, and forms the climax to, the revelation and its acceptance in faith.

This leads us to the question of the baptismal significance and reference of the incident; but before looking at this, and in order to do so more satisfactorily, we should examine the motifs which relate it to the gospel's wider context. The main theme to be taken up from the preceding chapters is that of Christ as the light of the world (9:5). The first level of meaning of the whole incident is based on this, and it receives further emphasis in the final words of the chapter: 'For judgment I came into this world, that those who do not see may see, and that those who see may become blind ... If you were blind, you would have no guilt; but now that you say "We see", you are indeed guilty' (9:39, 41). The lesson is that the true light coming into the world brings about the judgment which men force on themselves in response to Jesus. This is a theme which we have already seen recurring, and it is in fact part of the whole unravelling of the significance of the messianic age as made a reality in Jesus.

Another motif which would appear to be taken up from the feast of tabernacles (Jn 7 & 8), with all its messianic symbolism, is the reference to the pool of Siloam, for this played a major part in the ceremonies of the feast which were associated with water and new

life. Here we see the baptismal reference starting to
emerge. That this is explicit is indicated by the way in
which the name's (doubtful) etymology is mentioned;
'being sent' is an idea which the christian could not help
associating with Jesus himself, whom we have seen
insisting frequently that he is sent by his Father. The
resultant association of the waters of healing with
Christ's person has specific baptismal connotation. This
is brought out further in the dialogue.

The man born blind is being used as a universal
figure to represent the christian (but particularly the
Jewish christian) over against the unbelieving Jews, and
it is insisted upon that he was born blind through no fault
of his own. The comment in 9:3 might well be connected with the early understanding of the nature of
'original sin'; in Johannine thought real sin is the result
of failure in the face of the justice and confrontation
which Christ brings to the world. As the dialogue insists,
the healing achieved in the water is what brings the man
into this judgment-situation in which his faith develops
and he accepts the lordship and divinity of Jesus. The
phrase 'Lord, I believe' (9:38) has all the ring of a
baptismal *credo*; and certainly this passage was used
widely in the earliest documented baptismal ceremonies
of the church.

*1. Does the dialogue between the Jews and the man born blind
make as much sense when considered as an actual reported
incident, as it does when seen as a dramatic construction of the
evangelist? Which way of seeing it gives a better picture of the
real Jesus? What does 'the real Jesus' mean?*

*2. Can one compare believers and non-believers in the world
today with a man who has had his eyes opened and one who is still
blind?*

(ii) Jn 10:1–39. The good shepherd, the Son of God

At first sight the discourse that follows on the theme of 'the good shepherd' (10:1–21) has little to do with the scene which has preceded it. It would seem in fact that a completely new theme has been introduced. Obviously somewhere in the development of the gospel this must have been felt, for 10:6 is a comment on this situation and 10:7–18 is presented as the further explanation— though in fact it is very much more than this. Originally, however, 10:1–5 was probably continuous with 9:41, forming but a single speech. As we have seen, Jesus turns the judgment made by 'the Jews' on him back on to them, and this judgment continues by likening them to 'thieves and brigands' (10:1). The solemn formula with which the chapter opens: 'Truly, truly, I say to you' is frequently used to mark the beginning of a formal monologue, and would probably have been added when the rest of the discourse was appended to the original.

This whole passage, and the nature of the condemnation involved, can only be understood by reference to a passage in Ezekiel which is clearly being referred to here by the evangelist:

The word of the Lord came to me:
Son of man, prophesy against the shepherds of Israel,
prophesy and say to them, even to the shepherds,
> Thus says the Lord God:
> Ho, shepherds of Israel
> > who have been feeding yourselves!
> Should not shepherds feed the sheep?

(Ez 34:1, 2)

The denunciation proceeds in these terms throughout the chapter: instead of feeding the sheep the shepherds prey on them; they allow them to wander loose and be devoured by wild beasts. The shepherds will therefore be deposed and God himself will become shepherd of the flock. He will collect them together and lead them from exile. He will judge between them and he will know them and will set over them one shepherd, his servant David (ie the messiah) and they will experience all the character-istic conditions of the messianic age—plenty and fruit-fulness. The prophecy ends:

> They shall know
> > That I, the Lord their God,
> > am with them,
> And that they are my people ...
> And you are my sheep,
> > the sheep of my pasture.
> And I am your God,
> > > > says the Lord God.
> > > > > (Ez 34:30, 31)

The resemblance of this to Jn 10:1–18 is remarkable, and we can see how easily the condemnation of Ezekiel fits the adversaries of Jesus. Along with this the identification of Jesus with the promised messiah becomes clear: Jesus is the good shepherd promised in Ezekiel.

As the theme is developed here in Jn 10, however, it contains aspects which go beyond anything promised by Ezekiel. First of all the theme of life, which has been going hand in hand with the other themes throughout the gospel, is reintroduced (10:28). But not only does the good shepherd give life to his flock, he does this by laying down his own life in their defence (10:15). We have already had indications of how Jesus' conflict with the authorities is going to end in his death, but here we have the first explicit statement that he will in fact 'lay down his own life' so that he, through the power bestowed on him by his Father, 'may take it up again' (10:17) and thus share it with those who believe in him.

This ends the first major discourse of this chapter (Jn 10) with a description of the division amongst men which his words habitually bring about. There is a reference back to the opening of the eyes of the blind man (10:21) in order to bind the whole together. But at the same time the way is opened for the additional material which now follows. The theme of the good shepherd is reaffirmed within the context of messianic expectation, and what was hinted at just now as the source of Christ's life-giving power is explicitly asserted: 'I and the Father are one' (10:30).

In the separate material that follows this (10:34–38) there is an interesting style of argument which is perhaps more powerful than the straight logical progression which we tend to expect. On our presuppositions Jesus' argument about people being called gods looks like a complete prevarication; but it is in fact something quite different. The psalm quoted by Jesus (10:34) is referring, by way of castigation, to the unjust judges of Israel who are called 'gods' and 'sons of the Most High' (Ps 82:6) because they act on God's behalf, yet will die because of their infidelity. The implication is that if they are called gods because they mediate God's judgment, how much more is he, the righteous judge of Israel (the good shepherd), entitled to this claim.

This claim, however, depends on the power he receives from the Father; but he has in fact become the full location of this power because he has been consecrated as himself the temple (10:36). We have already seen Jesus as the bread of life replacing the passover manna (Jn 6) and as the light and life of the world replacing the symbolism of the feast of tabernacles (Jn

7 & 8), and now at the feast of the dedication of the temple (10:22) Jesus is indicated once again as replacing this latter (cf 2:19–21). It is only if Jesus betrays his Father that he is worthy of condemnation, and he calls on the people to acknowledge that his works (which are his Father's works—and this does not simply mean 'good deeds' but the whole fulfilment of God's salvific work which he is manifesting in his signs, actions and words) witness to his fidelity. Again the discourse terminates with the assertion that the Father and Jesus have unique and totally intimate relationship.

1. Does Jesus' presence in the world amongst his disciples still force men into bringing judgment upon themselves as it did during his ministry?

2. Does the judgment bear only on those outside the church— ie the 'world'—or does it reflect on the church itself?

3. Is Christ still speaking to us through Ezekiel?

Jn 11:1–12:53. The climax of the ministry
(i) Jn 11:1–54. The raising of Lazarus

The two chapters of the 'book of signs' which remain have peculiarities which suggest that they are in fact editorial additions to the original gospel material. In the light of this the words at the end of the preceding chapter (10:40–42) look as if they are in effect the conclusion to the presentation of the ministry: Jesus goes back across Jordan to where John has been baptising—in other words the ministry is brought full circle, and whereas he found no faith in him amongst his own people, those of Transjordania accepted him as being precisely what John had proclaimed. This reflects, on the one hand, the way in which the evangelist sees Jesus as fulfilling the whole prophetic tradition, and on the other hand the way in which the church had become established outside Judaea, rather than at its centre.

Two features indicate that the two chapters that follow are additional material. First of all there is a subtle difference in vocabulary and usage of terminology. The most notable is the way in which the term 'the Jews', which has almost consistently been used to indicate the Jewish authorities (especially, we have surmised, the pharisees) is now in these chapters used simply to designate the Jewish people. The polemic connotation has vanished.

Secondly, the material itself, together with the part which it plays in the gospel, indicates that it has been added and has as a result displaced material once occupying its place. The whole story of Lazarus comes into this category. The raising of Lazarus is presented here as the reason for the authorities taking the final step in deciding to do away with Jesus. There are good theological reasons for its presentation in this way, but the narrative account in the synoptics is in a sense far more realistic: it was the cleansing of the temple by Jesus that brought about the final showdown.

It has been suggested that the whole Lazarus story is an allegorical invention of the fourth evangelist, and is built up out of a number of incidents recounted in the synoptics. Such a theory is based on the assumption that there is no valid independent traditional material or historicity in John. We have seen how this represents an old-fashioned liberal view which has no basis in reality. These days we have to take Johannine material more seriously.

The raising of Lazarus only really becomes a problem in conflict with the (assumed) more accurate accounts in the synoptics when we fail to understand the nature of the fourth evangelist's presentation of his material. At one level of 'truth' the cleansing of the temple was very likely the last straw. If we remain at this level the full story of Lazarus looks rather unlikely. We have, however, seen enough of the pattern of Johannine thought (whether it belongs to the original or later authors involved in the gospel) to understand what is being said here. It was indeed because Jesus stood for 'the resurrection and the life' (11:25) in opposition to the authorities who by now in their reaction to Jesus were standing for the principle of death and darkness, that they were forced to bring the judgment on themselves to bear unjustly upon their accuser, and judge, and attempt to destroy him—an attempt which in fact, in its 'success', brought about the full flowing of the life which he had to offer.

John seems to have taken this one miracle, which in the synoptic tradition had not registered sufficiently to survive the transmission and development involved (there are other raising miracles in the synoptics) and has blown it up in this climactic way to bring forth, more powerfully than in any of the synoptic accounts, the basic reason why Jesus' ministry led to his death. It thus has dramatic as well as theological significance.

Two general points about this additional material (Jn 11 & 12) need to be made before we can look at it in any closer detail. First of all we should notice the way in which it is not just 'stuck on' to the preceding chapters; in 11:37, for example, this incident and the healing of the blind man are bound together by a remark made by the crowd. There is in fact a considerable similarity between these signs in themselves and in their presentation; one is the dramatisation of the theme of Jesus as the light of the world, and the other a dramatisation of the

theme which has been running concurrently with it—
Jesus as the life of men. At the same time, however, we
should notice the difference in style of dramatic presentation. Here, in this new section, we do not have a clear
case of a sign followed by a discourse, but a mixture of the
two. The dramatic style, though equally powerful, is less
developed, less intricate, because as we have seen (eg
chs 7 & 8 and 9 & 10) the former technique to a large
extent embodies the latter and adds to it. This new
section would thus appear to have had less development
in the tradition before being taken up and incorporated
into the material which had, however, received some
form of earlier actual written expression. (This might
interestingly account for the difference of usage with
regard to the term 'the Jews' which has already been
mentioned.)

The theological and narrative aspects of this episode
are so closely interrelated that it is not really possible to
extract anything as definitely belonging to the one rather
than the other. But we should be aware of the nature of
the questions that ought to be put with regard to the
text. Some will be more orientated towards the narrative
aspect, others towards the theological, and yet others
towards the interrelation of these two. For example,
when thinking of the setting, both personal and loca-
tional, it is significant that the synoptics do mention that
when Jesus went to Jerusalem he lodged at Bethany
(Mt 26:6 etc). We should note that the synoptics have
no account of more than one visit by Jesus to Jerusalem (apart from the Lucan infancy narratives) and
little material, referring to the ministry, outside
Galilee.

On the other hand we should note the specifically
theological orientation which is given by 11:4, which is

to be compared with 9:3, but there is also an interesting couplet a little later which adds a different dimension. In 11:4 Lazarus' sickness (and what is to follow) is for the glory of God, and of the Son; in 11:15 his death is to be welcomed for the sake of the apostles' (the church's?) faith. This passage (11:11–15), which contains a characteristic (though not very weighty) *double entendre*, would seem to have been conveniently inserted into other material dealing exclusively with the need for Jesus to go up to Jerusalem and confront his enemies. It is possible to see the way in which a number of different themes are being woven together. Finally, in this section of the 'narrative', one should note the possible ecclesial reference in 11:11 where 'our friend' (RSV) should read 'our beloved'—a typically early christian form of address for the fellow christian. This may well introduce yet a further level at which the story is meant to be understood.

Jesus' meeting with Martha (11:18–27) is paralleled by his meeting with Mary (11:28–33) in such a way that one can be almost sure the one or the other has been added to the text in its development. The encounter with Martha is the richer by far, and that with Mary really adds little or nothing. Which is original and which has been added? If the original had been improved on by adding Martha's meeting it would have been odd, for Martha, by comparison with Mary, is rather unimportant (if we are to accept a relation between the Johannine and synoptic presentations). It seems more likely that Martha's meeting is part of the traditional material and Mary's has been added in order to give her a role in this scene. This also has the effect of tying this episode in with the opening scene of the next chapter.

Martha's meeting follows the familiar pattern of an

increasing faith given impetus by an initial misunderstanding and fed with the words of Christ. These words
throw the emphasis from a future eschatology to a
realised one: the resurrection and the life are here and
now for the believer in Christ. Martha expresses her
faith in characteristic terms, but that this faith is as yet
far from adequate is indicated by the continued disbelief
in front of the tomb (11:39, 40). It takes the miracle
to clinch it. One can detect here a theology rather more
akin to that of the synoptics than any we have seen so
far in John. The sign here comes at the end of the discourse rather than at its beginning; this seems to pre-
figure the way in which the farewell discourse precedes
the sign of the crucifixion and resurrection.

Leading up to the actual raising of Lazarus many of
the earlier themes are brought together and epitomised.
'See how he loved him' (11:36) cannot but recall the
way in which the Father has so loved the world as to
send his only-begotten son to men; the reference to the
healing of the blind man (11:37) joins together the ideas
of Jesus as the life and as the light of the world; in 11:40
faith in Jesus is related to the manifestation of God's
glory. One cannot help seeing that as both an inclusive
reference back from this, the last miracle of the book of
signs, to the first miracle at Cana (cf 2:11) and as a
forward reference to Jesus' glorification.

Before raising Lazarus from the dead Jesus prays to
his Father (11:41, 42). It has been said (cleverly and
brutally) that he is in fact simply 'praying to the
gallery'. But one can only say something like this if in a
sense one is taking this description too literally. In this
'prayer' is to be found the expression of the relationship
between Jesus and his Father which has been expressed
and developed throughout the ministry—and this

relationship can, in its profoundest form, itself be called prayer. It is precisely because of this relationship that Jesus is himself the resurrection and the life of men, and it is thus that he can shout out in a loud voice (ie to all men): 'Lazarus come out' (11:43). The whole dramatic presentation, with its layer upon layer of theological implication, is masterly.

The rest of the chapter (11:45–57) describes the effect of Jesus' ministry on the authorities and the people as it reaches its climax. The scene is set for his final going up to Jerusalem to suffer and to die.

1. Can one detect signs of artificiality in the story of the raising of Lazarus? What sort of artificiality might be involved? Does artificiality mean unreality?

2. Are we meant to take this whole story literally or figuratively? or can we in some way have both of these together?

3. Has the evangelical editor significantly altered the overall meaning of Jesus' ministry by adding this extra section on to its original presentation in chs 2–10?

(ii) Jn 12:1–50. Jesus goes up to Jerusalem

(*a*) *Jn 12:1–8. The anointing at Bethany*

Before Jesus' final entry into Jerusalem we have this scene in which he is anointed. Some commentators have seen this as a 'royal anointing' before the triumphant ride into Jerusalem, but in fact neither event has this characteristic. We are told explicitly that the anointing was in preparation for his burial, and it is clear that Jesus is going up to Jerusalem as a very different kind of king from the one expected by the people.

The scene of the anointing presents a number of problems. It is very similar to the account of the same

incident in Mark (Matthew is simply copying Mark)
though it has some notable differences. Mark's account
is the more convincing as a narrative: Mary anoints
the head of Jesus with ointment. In John she anoints his
feet and then wipes it off with her hair—an odd thing
to do in any situation. What seems to have happened
is that there has been some cross-fertilisation here from
Luke's gospel—partly on account of similar terminology
in each case, and partly on account of the theological
perspectives involved. In Luke (7:36–50) a sinful woman
comes and weeps on Jesus' feet and immediately wipes
them with her hair. These features seem to have been
imported into John's account, whilst everything else
about it is so similar to Mark (though with inessential
differences) as to indicate that John and Mark were
originally dependent upon the same traditional source.
One should note that as the result of all this there has
been a long-perpetuated confusion in the church between
Mary of Bethany, the sinful woman of Capernaum (Lk
7:37) and Mary Magdalene, who have been rolled
together into one repentant sinner who loved Jesus.

The theological significance of the scene is basically
the same as in Mark—namely Jesus' burial is being prefigured. However, the way in which it is presented in
John, as the result of his mixing the two stories together,
is that Mary, in her increasing faith and love, was per-
forming an unconscious prophetic action whilst at the
same time the Jewish authorities, who have just been
presented as deciding to kill Jesus (11:49–53), were
expressing the culmination of their rejection and hatred.
These two movements, of faith and rejection, can as a
result be seen to be converging on the same point—the
death and glorification of Jesus.

The phrase 'Let her keep it (the ointment) for the

day of my burial' (12:7) is highly elliptical in the Greek
and has obviously given trouble as there are interpreta-
tive alternative readings in the earliest sources. It
would seem to indicate the way in which unknowingly
she had in fact kept it until now for the purpose of
(symbolically) embalming Jesus' body. The phrase 'The
poor you have always with you' (12:8) is a scribal
addition recalling the traditional twofold works of mercy
which were always binding on men: first to bury the
dead (piety) and secondly to feed the poor (charity). It
is not, as historically it has often and tragically been
taken, an indication that this state of affairs, ie the
existence of a class of poor, is God's will for the world!

(b) *Jn 12:9–19. The entry into Jerusalem*

In the synoptic gospels the ride into Jerusalem is the
climax of the ministry. For them this is the first time
that Jesus goes up to Jerusalem and he is shown as the
messiah coming to claim his heritage—capital and temple
(the 'cleansing of the temple' follows this in the synoptic
accounts). In John the same material is retained, though
in abbreviated or less developed form, but its significance
is rather different. The climax of the ministry (or rather
its epitomisation) has been expressed in the raising of
Lazarus, and this is what is depicted as leading to the
events which follow. Every effort is made by the evangelical editor to tie these two together. Chapter 12 is to a
large extent a collection of bits and pieces keeping this
continuity going, though it reaches its climax in the next
section (12:20–36). Note the way in which reference to
Lazarus is made again and again (12:9 & 17) to keep
this 'jointing' alive and dynamic. The anointing of Jesus
by Mary also looks as if one of its main roles were that of
continuity in a similar way.

The entry into Jerusalem, however, has far more theological significance (as one might expect) than these remarks have indicated. Naturally what is significant is the way in which the quotation from Zechariah (Jn 12:15), which is also found in Matthew's account, is interpreted. But let us start with Jesus' reaction to the way in which the crowds proclaim him as messiah with 'Hosanna' and 'Blessed is he who comes in the name of the Lord' (Ps 118:26). The palm fronds (12:13), although associated with the feasts of tabernacles and the dedication, have even stronger Maccabean nationalistic associations. We seem to have another case of the way in which the crowd gets the wrong idea about Jesus as messiah, similar to that in 6:15 after the multiplication of loaves.

In that case Jesus simply hid himself from them; here we are told that he gets on a donkey and rides on it. This is an interesting reaction, for it represents a significant reversal of the order presented in the synoptics. The meaning of this action, as it is presented in John, is given to us in the quotation from Zechariah, but it would not here seem to indicate humility, as it does for Matthew, for that motif which is to be found in Zechariah is not included here. Matthew used it (Mt 21:5) and it would have been available to John whatever the source of his tradition. The significance of the prophecy for John is something different.

The clue to its meaning is given by the mixed reference in the first line of the quotation. Zechariah says: 'Rejoice greatly, daughter of Zion ...' (Zech 9:9) not: 'Fear not, daughter of Zion' (Jn 12:15). The phrase used by John seems to be a reference to Zephaniah (3:16) where the phrase 'even the king of Israel', added by John to the psalm quoted in 12:13, also seems to come from. We can see the evangelist steadily bending our attention away from the idea of a nationalistic king messiah, and turning it to the picture of the messiah given in the Zephaniah prophecy.

This tells Israel that the Lord, the King of Israel, is in their midst, and that to Jerusalem, filled with his presence, people from all over the world will stream for refuge. The Lord will save them from their enemies, gathering together the outcasts and the cripples. Thus Jesus' gift of life to men, epitomised in the raising of Lazarus, is to be understood not nationalistically, but universally; not for the elite, but for the outcasts. Here we have echoes of a theme often repeated in the synoptics.

This understanding of the prophecy is backed up by the way in which the pharisees (without knowing its full significance) say: 'Look, the world has gone after him' (12:19); and immediately following this we are told that at the feast 'Greeks' come wanting to see Jesus. Finally in 12:32 Jesus declares that when he is lifted up from the earth, he will draw all men to himself. Despite the fragmentary nature of so much of the material in this chapter the theological motifs are as powerful, and as characteristically Johannine, as ever.

(c) *Jn 12:20–36. 'The hour has come'*

Here at last in this whole section (Jn 11 & 12) we have a discourse fulfilling the same sort of role as the major discourses we have seen earlier. The reference back, however, is greater than to just the earlier part of this section, and so is the reference forward; nevertheless as it appears it forms the climax of the train of thought which we have just been following—that of the messiah's relationship to the gentiles—and indeed, along with the raising of

Lazarus, though in a very different manner, it forms the climax of the whole section, and in fact the climax of the public ministry. Now for the first time, having several times been told the opposite, we are told that at last the hour has come (12:23); and the coming of the 'Greeks' and the coming of the hour go hand in hand together.

The Greeks referred to are gentile proselytes, not hellenistic Jews (the Greek term is different in each case). Probably some vague and half-remembered incident is being recalled here, but so strong is the theological orientation that these Greeks, having come, seem to slip away, like Nicodemus did in his dialogue with Jesus, without one's knowing whether they actually met Jesus or not. Starting with the proclamation that the hour has come the development of the theme proceeds without reference to the Greeks who sparked it off.

The glorification of the Son of Man, for which the hour has come, means his death, and what immediately follows here has a striking similarity to the prayer of Jesus to his Father in the garden of Gethsemane (which is not recounted in John):

The hour has come	12:23
for the Son of Man to be glorified	
Now is my soul troubled.	27
And what shall I say,	
'Father, save me from this hour'?	
No, for this purpose I have come to this hour.	
Father, glorify thy name.	28
Then a voice came from heaven ...	
The crowd standing by heard it ...	29

You will have noticed that we have left out 12:24–26. This section seems to have been made up of other material and neatly inserted here. The words are more than appropriate but do tend to lessen the wider reference which as a result can be more easily missed. These verses have marked similarity with sayings recorded in the synoptics. The first verse (12:24), given the context, is referring to Jesus himself; the second (12:25) refers to his disciples—not only must he die but so also must they. The third verse (12:26) refers to how these two are related; we only need to add the words 'take up his cross' and the similarity with Mark 8:34 is complete. The final sentence of the passage tells of the reward that Jesus gives to his servants, and reiterates the continuous assertion that the life he shares with men is the life he shares with the Father.

But to return to the theme of the 'garden of Gethsemane'. One ought to be aware of the fact that the prayer in the garden, as related in the synoptics, is obviously a dramatic construction derived from the many sayings of Christ which were handed on in the early church—it could hardly have been a pure invention or surmise. Here in John we have what must be a very similar sort of construction in a rather different, though in many ways dramatically as climactic, context. The drama is heightened by the voice from heaven, the people's comment and Jesus' answer (12:28–32). Also, just as the synoptics do, this version stresses the struggling human nature of Jesus in the face of the mounting oppression of Satan. The 'dualism' which we have seen from time to time in John here reaches its starkest proportions. It is at the moment of Jesus' death that his glory is completed and his judgment bears most forcefully on the world, dividing it between darkness and light, evil and truth.

The triumph of life over death, and the giving of life to all men, is to be found in the 'lifting up' of Jesus. This phrase (12:32) is deliberately ambiguous in John.

It refers both to the crucifixion and to the resurrection and ascension. In John's eyes these are not just events which happened one after the other, but temporally extended expressions of the one reality: the death of Christ, in which he lays down himself for all men, is itself the triumph over death, and is therefore itself the resurrection. This resurrection is equally the shared life of the Father and the Son and so implies the ascension. But in this being-lifted-up we have been drawn to him (12:32), and the distinction between heaven and earth has now vanished; there remains, as a radical distinction, only that between turning away from Christ and turning to him.

This whole idea of the triumphant crucifixion, especially as expressed in these terms, probably has its origins in the suffering servant poems of deutero-Isaiah:

> Behold, my servant shall prosper.
> > he shall be exalted and lifted up,
> > and shall be very high.
> As many were astounded at him—
> > his appearance was so marred . . .
> Surely he has borne our griefs
> > and carried our sorrow. (Is 52:13, 14;
> > > > > 53:4)

It is also very interesting in view of what follows (in John's gospel) that there is a close association here with the theme of light:

> You are my servant . . .
> > in whom I will be glorified.
> I will give you as a light to the nations
> > that my salvation may reach
> > the ends of the earth. (Is 49:3, 6)

For at this point in the discourse (after a moment of

'confusion' at 12:34, in which 'being lifted up' and 'the Son of Man' are associated, as they have been throughout so far) the argument is immediately concluded with reference to the light, which is Christ, and the darkness, which is his absence. There are possibly overtones of Qumran theology here and of christian baptism (seen as enlightenment—cf Jn 9). But dramatically this ending leads straight into the last supper discourse and the death of Jesus.

In fact, however, it does not! There has been added a summary evaluation of Jesus' public ministry and a summary proclamation by Jesus himself.

(d) Jn 12:37–50. Summary of the public ministry

Here, at the end of the 'book of signs', the author pauses to evaluate the effect of the ministry: 'though he had done so many signs before them, yet they did not believe in him ... nevertheless many even of the authorities believed in him ... [yet] they loved the praise of men more than the praise of God' (12:37, 42, 43). Here is the irony of it all: 'He has blinded their eyes and hardened their heart, lest they should see with their eyes and perceive with their heart and turn to me to heal them' (12:40—Is 6:10). Despite the manner of its presentation, with its acceptance of the inevitability of the fulfilment of the prophecies, this is not the expression of a rigid determinism, but in fact an invitation to believe.

The 'causality' involved here is one which Jesus, in fulfilling the prophetic movement in his own person, takes on himself. And, as we have seen, in the Johannine mind it is the confrontation with Jesus himself which brings upon men the judgment which is their own. This is not an easy concept to understand, and we have to experience it again and again in the gospel in order, gradually, to begin to appreciate it. Perhaps here in this passage we have one of its most elliptical formulations.

The proclamation of Jesus which immediately follows (12:44–50) contains the same idea (12:48) though with an emphasis which has elements of future rather than realised eschatology. This time, however, it is set within a more hopeful and encouraging context. Christ is standing there as a witness of the light and the life and the truth which he embodies. He is standing there as it were with open arms to welcome those who receive him, and come into his light out of their darkness. His final affirmation is that he is the source of life precisely because he has come to us at the will of the Father. The invitation is wide open for us also to accept this will.

1. Is humility and the refusal of all positions of honour and regality an absolute essential for the church to present itself as embodying a message of life for the whole world? Do grandeur and pomp play a valid part in the church's presentation of Christ to the world? Do we indulge in this in the wrong way? Can we afford to? What are we going to do about it, and what can be done about it?

2. Is it essentially morbid to see the triumph over evil as only being achieved through physical suffering? To what extent is the real humanity of Jesus brought out here? or is it presented too theologically to be real?

3. His ministry seems to present a wide-open invitation to all men to come to Christ and know life and truth in him—or at least this is how the evangelist presents it. Does its actual presentation make it available to all men? Can it confront them and communicate with them simply as it stands, or does it need 'translation' and 'de-mythologization' into different cultural formats? How can this be done without misrepresenting the message?

3

The final hour
Jn 13:1–20:31

Introduction

The second major section of the gospel, consisting of chapters 13–20, can be called prosaically 'The last days', or more theologically, reflecting the theme of the preceding chapter, 'The final hour'. Even more imaginatively, and certainly correctly from a theological point of view, it can be (and has been) called 'The book of glory' to match the appellation of the earlier section as 'The book of signs'. As, however, we were prosaic there and entitled that section 'The public ministry', we will settle here for 'The final hour' remembering that in the mind of the evangelist the events of these days and the days after the resurrection are a temporally extended expression of what is fundamentally one reality, the 'glorification', rather than an historical series of incidents. Thus in choosing this title rather than the even more prosaic 'The last days' we are laying stress on what seems to be an important theme in this section of the gospel.

This second half of the gospel is something clearly distinct from the earlier parts. It is in a sense self-contained and has a distinctive format of its own. It is nevertheless as fundamentally Johannine, in both thought, language and literary construction, as any other part of the gospel. It does, however, contain more material put in by the final redactor (quite apart from his 'epilogue', chapter 21, which is outside the structure of this section anyway) than is to be found in the earlier chapters. The material coming from this redactor is quite easy to spot because, unlike earlier editors of the gospel, he regards the material already written as sacrosanct. Nowhere does he edit or alter in order to graft in a new section or rearrange something; what he does is to add and insert complete passages (or comments) without more than slightly disturbing the sequence of the original material. It is for this reason that he has been consistently referred to as a 'redactor' rather than as an 'editor', this latter term being reserved for the earlier author or authors who have manipulated, reformed or reconstructed the original literary formulation. Where the redactor has made major additions to the text as he had it we tend to come across noticeable disorientations or breaks in the 'argument', or in the structure; though to be fair one must say that these are in no way incongruous—his insertions are handled with delicacy and intelligence.

Before indicating where it is to be found and what effect it has had on the general shape of the gospel, it should be mentioned that this added material is in no immediate way basically different from the original, nor is it necessarily of later provenance. Quite often it has a similarity, or partial similarity, to material in the original gospel of such a nature as to suggest that what we have here is the same traditional material developed within the same community in a slightly different way. The original evangelist was obviously selective (cf Jn 20:30) using only material which suited his homiletical/catechetical/apologetic purpose. The final redactor, as a member of the same community (his style and interests cannot be explained otherwise), has had available to him a whole lot of other material; some of this might already have been written down, some may have been liturgical formulae, hymns, etc. At least some of this he has felt also to be relevant to the overall presentation of the gospel, and has thus added it, without (as we have seen) actually altering the original formulation.

The book of glory in its original form probably had the following bipartite structure:

1. The last supper, consisting of an account of the washing of the feet (and probably in its earliest form some sort of reference to the eucharistic institution); followed by a farewell speech, of a formalised nature, to his disciples by Jesus.

   These are still to be found as a unit in chapters 13 and 14; and this intimate section effectively formed the 'discourse' which constituted the 'commentary' on what followed.

2. An account of the arrest, trial, crucifixion and resurrection, contained in chapters 18, 19, 20.

To this, apart from the epilogue (Jn 21), the redactor has added a number of extra 'farewell speeches'. The result is that the greater part of the farewell discourse as we know it is additional material, which has had a very considerable effect on its overall balance. We have re-marked earlier how, in this second half of the gospel, the discourse material has to precede rather than follow the action. Such an order is not only dramatically correct at this point, but it is also the case that in the last supper, whatever exactly went on there, this 'commentary' had in effect already been initiated by Christ himself. Not only is the discourse at the supper a comment on the final hour, but the supper itself fulfils this role; it is the pointing of the significance of the moment of glorification.

The material added by the redactor has a similar nature, but since it is all reflecting back on the death and resurrection from a later period, summing up various aspects of that complex event, it tends towards a certain abstraction from the actual physical drama; and this is exacerbated by its being additional material. The overall result of this is twofold; first of all it upsets the dramatic balance and as a result reduces the impact of the events which follow—one already knows too many of the 'answers'; and secondly it has an effect on us similar to that which can be produced by studying, or even reading, the prologue before the rest of the gospel (cf pp 31–35) —again we are acquainted with too many of the 'answers' too soon.

From the point of view of the redactor the place where he inserted this material was the obvious one; it was quite customary to add farewell speech upon farewell speech at the conclusion of a work. The original farewell speech thus determined the position of the insertions. Nevertheless from our point of view this material is better considered along with the prologue (to which some of it has considerable similarity) in our conclusion. We lose nothing by this because the original version was dramatically effective, and theologically more than adequate; and in a study of scripture such as this present one I think we gain quite a lot by it.

Up to now we have only once or twice been dealing with anything which is also explicitly presented by the synoptics. From here on the Johannine and synoptic accounts run side by side, and as a result comparison between them becomes more and more necessary. This comparison, however, involves an enormous amount of scholarly work, because there are some profound inconsistencies between the accounts. The whole day-by-day dating, for example, in the synoptic and Johannine accounts is different, and this difference has considerable theological implications.

The details of the scholarship involved in untangling this problem are not something with which we can our-selves become entangled. The arguments for and against a particular position can be given only occasionally; otherwise the appropriate sources will be indicated. The present author will simply have to outline what he judges to be the most satisfactory solution to such prob-lems, giving indications of the strength of the arguments involved, and then present the gospel accordingly.

One further point should be made whilst on this subject. For a number of reasons, both historical and cultural, people have tended to take the synoptics' account of the last supper, the trial, the death and the resurrection of Jesus as the 'historically accurate one'. In fact all along they tend to judge John against the synoptics, assuming the former to be 'unworldly', 'out of touch with reality'—a spiritualisation of the gospel message—and to look for 'reality', for the 'actual Jesus of history', in the latter. Modern scholarship, coming on (and sometimes treading on) the heels of the liberalism which effectively enhanced some aspects of this outlook, is beginning to show how false a picture it is.

The Johannine authors themselves would also have been amongst the first to deny the concept of 'spiritual-ity' which this view embodies; the whole of the fourth gospel stands against it. As we have seen in the earlier part of this commentary, the dramatic presentation which John gives to his material—material which is beginning to be recognised as equally authentic as, and sometimes more accurate than, that behind the synoptics—is not a movement away from it but an expression of its most profound reality and a deepening of its impact. The same is true of this second half of the gospel, and whilst we are exploring it we should keep an entirely open mind about its 'accuracy', without being misled by our inherited presuppositions deriving from the synoptic accounts. If they witness three to one against John it is quite simply because they are in collusion. If their evidence seems in any way more 'real' it is because our sense of what constitutes reality is sadly impoverished. In this area we have a great deal to learn from John.

Jn 13:1–14:31. The last supper
(i) Jn 13:1–30. At the meal
(a) *A passover meal or not?*

We can make no immediate judgment on their significance, but the first thing to do is to notice the differences between the Johannine and the synoptic accounts of the last supper. In John there is no description of any preparation for the meal, and there is no explicit suggestion that it is in fact a passover meal. There is no account of the eucharistic institution such as 'He took bread, and blessed, and broke it, and gave it to them and said, "Take; this is my body . . ."' (Mk 14:22). On the positive side by contrast we have, first of all, the assertion that the time was in fact 'before the feast of the passover' (13:1). As, however, the mention of the actual meal follows extremely abruptly (13:2) we cannot be certain that there was always any direct connection. (Jn 13:1 looks as if it is an introduction to this whole section added by the redactor when he added chapters 15–17; though it could have been added when 13:21–30 was introduced—see below.)

The main item in John's account which is not to be

found in the synoptics is, of course, the description of Jesus' washing the feet of the disciples (though there are possibly hints of it to be found in Lk 22:27). Finally in John there is added to the supper a farewell discourse, though this need not concern us in the present context, because it is simply a characteristic instance of the way in which John adds discourse to action. With regard to the elements which are common to John and one or other of the synoptics, and there are quite a number of small but interesting points common in this way, the differences of expression seem to indicate that John and the synoptics have independent sources of tradition; there is, however, as there is throughout the gospel, a slightly closer relationship with Luke than with the other synoptics.

If, as mentioned, there is the possibility of something missing from in front of 13:2, then it is just possible that Jesus was celebrating an anticipated passover. Also it is just possible that he and his disciples were using a different calendar (a Qumran one?) from the official one. But these suggestions, though ingenious, can in no way be proved, and in fact they introduce more difficulties than they eliminate. If we discount them, then, we have to say that, according to John, Jesus and his disciples were not celebrating the passover meal, for the gospel explicitly tells us that the passover was the following day, insisting as it does that Jesus was condemned to death at the moment when the passover 'victims' were being slaughtered, and that he died on the passover. Of course, for the moment at any rate, on account of the obviously strong theological motifs here, we can make no immediate comment on the historicity of this assertion; we simply have to conclude that for John, unlike the synoptics, the last supper was not a passover.

The whole of the Johannine chronology has been

challenged, most notably by J. Jeremias (*Eucharistic Words of Jesus*), because of his certainty that the last supper was a passover meal. His reasoning is sound as far as it goes, but it leads him into a number of improbabilities in his interpretation of the events that follow. What he is failing to notice is the possible difference between its being the passover supper, and its being *presented* as that. The later chronology of the trial and death of Jesus fits in most easily with John's account, and it is far from inconceivable that, with the strong paschal associations of the whole incident, the synoptic tradition connected it with the prefigurement of Christ's death rather than with that death itself. It is not at all impossible that, as a result, the eucharistic institution got developed and written up within the dramatic context of a passover meal, which was then of course identified with the meal which Jesus and his disciples shared the day before he died.

All this is of course speculation, but its purpose is to show that the presentation of the last supper by the synoptics as a passover meal cannot be taken to prove that their chronology, rather than John's, is correct. There is nothing, apart from historical prejudice, to indicate that the synoptics are more 'trustworthy' with regard to 'accurate narrative' here, and there is some evidence (cf R. E. Brown, *The Gospel according to John*, pp 555–557) which favours John in this respect.

If we accept that in the Johannine account the last supper is not a passover meal, does this affect our understanding of eucharistic theology in any fundamental way?

(*b*) *Jn 13:1–20. The washing of the feet*
The first thing to look at is the overall structure of the

incident, leaving till later the incidental details which do,
however, have a bearing on our interpretation. The first
basic unit (13:3–5) is a description of Jesus' action: he
lays down his garments, pours water into a pitcher (not
'a basin', RSV) and washes his disciples' feet. There
follows (13:6–11) a dialogue between Jesus and Peter
which represents in dramatic form the significance of
Jesus' actions—one should note that it has many of the
characteristics of a Johannine construction and cannot
be regarded as simple reporting. Jesus then takes up his
clothes and resumes his place. (The Greek words for
laying down and taking up his clothes are the same as
those used for laying down and taking up his life. This is
not without significance because the whole of this scene
is set within such a context. Cf 13:1, 2 & 3.)

When the action and dialogue are complete there
follows (13:12–20) a discourse which in fact plays the
part of a reinterpretation of the scene. This has a number
of extremely interesting aspects to it. It is clearly a later
addition since the first 'explanation' is organically related
to the action, and it would seem to be the work of an
editor, not the final redactor, because there has been
some not inconsiderable shifting and alteration of the
original material in the area of 13:10 & 11, and probably in 13:21. There are also indications of similar
interleaving, rather than addition, in 13:19. In 13:18
there is a reference to 'eating my bread' and the word
used here for 'eat' only occurs elsewhere in this gospel
in the section on the bread of life discourse which, as was
pointed out, was specifically eucharistic, and which was
also an obvious editorial addition. It was also pointed
out there that this addition seemed to contain elements
of the 'eucharistic institution'. It would seem most
probable that the hand responsible for introducing the

specifically eucharistic material into chapter 6 is the
same as that which provided an alternative interpretation
of the foot-washing in chapter 13.

Having assembled all this evidence we can now
attempt an interpretation of the 'incident'—ie the
Johannine last supper—taking into account both what it
contains and what it omits. We have noted the way in
which it is set closely in the context of Jesus' death, and it
appears that the action itself indicates the reason for,
and the ultimate nature of, that death. The placing of
the theme of betrayal both before (13:2) and after it
(13:10b/11) emphasises this. Other indications of its
significance are given by the reference to the Father's
having given all things into Jesus' hands, for this refers
to his salvific work now reaching its critical point.

The first interpretation of the action (13:6–10) stresses
that it is Jesus who 'needs' to perform this task of humility
for the sake of the salvation of men rather than their feeling
the need of it; or rather that their need is that he should
do it (cf 13:8, and the whole of the 'misunderstanding'
between Peter and Jesus 13:8–10). Again, what is being
symbolised is that this is the moment, sparked off by
Judas' betrayal, when Jesus sums up the whole of the
life which he has shared with his disciples and lays it
down on their behalf so that they might share it with him.
The constant reiteration of the betrayal motif indicates
also that this is the dark side of the death-in-which-
death-is-conquered. The conquering is only achieved in
battle to the death with Satan and his forces; but Jesus
is taking this on willingly (13:18) to fulfil his mission.

The 'second explanation' of the footwashing (13:12–
20) is in many ways simpler. It holds the action up as a
model for christian behaviour, and would seem to
represent a less 'sacramental' interpretation of Jesus'

action. The themes of the church's mission (13:16) and her struggle against evil (13:18) are both suggested, and are related to the exemplary aspects of Jesus' action. The theme of his death is not missing either; it would be impossible to dissociate 'I tell you this now, before it takes place, that when it does take place you may believe that I am' (13:19—'I am he', RSV, falsely weakens the whole sense) from 'When you have lifted up the Son of Man, then you will know that I am' (8:28); the uses of the 'I am' formula in this absolute sense are not after all as common as all that.

If we are right in thinking that this passage is associated with the additional eucharistic material in the bread of life discourse it is necessary to discern a higher motivation than any indicated by the above commentary for its inclusion, and for the possible displacement of material from this context to that. We are in danger of pure speculation here, but the following is not entirely without basis in the evidence as we have it, and does open the way to a deeper understanding of John's account of the last supper.

It is quite possible that when the Johannine account of the last supper, which gives prominence to the footwashing ceremony, began to emerge in literary form it came into conflict with the specifically eucharistic presentation of Christ's last hours which had spread abroad early in the church. The addition of the material which we have seen above would effectively play down the sacramental nature of the footwashing. At the same time the transference of the eucharistic material (which we do not consider to have been as highly developed here as in the synoptics) from this context to that of the bread of life discourse would have had the effect of giving greater weight to its sacramental nature.

One would only assume the opposite to be true if one had in one's hands, at the time, one of the synoptic gospels.

This particular shift of material, over against any other shift, would also have the advantage of fully respecting the insights and understanding of the gospel message as expressed in the original form of the work. All of this presupposes an editor working on the gospel, within its true tradition, at some period after its original formulation, yet prior to the work of the final redactor— a supposition which accords well with the theory of composition outlined in the introduction. If this is acceptable, it would seem that, contrary to the views expressed by a number of commentators, the sacramental slant given to the original gospel is earlier than the work of the final redactor and continuous, at least, with the spirit of the original.

Now we can return to John's presentation of the last supper and see that it is in effect every bit as powerful, and possibly as accurate, a description of that occasion as are the descriptions in the synoptics. In fact with regard to actual chronology it may easily be that John is the more accurate. What concerns us at this moment, however, is not so much the factual accuracy as the full historical reality. What we can now see is how *each* account of the last supper represents the full dimensions of the way in which Christ's life, shared with those whom he called to him, was brought at that moment to a climax of self-giving, death and resurrection. Both accounts are symbolic and dramatic representations of the point of focus of that life through which all his disciples have to pass to achieve the resurrection; both contain the fullness of God's presence to us in Christ, that is its full reality. They are in fact, both of them, the eucharist in its institution.

That one rather than the other has taken a path central to the church's sacramental life and awareness may be accident or may be because it contains more powerful and cogent symbolism. As long as it has become a full expression of the reality it does not matter. But as we habitually fail to realise this in its fullness, it is possible that the appreciation of John's contribution here could help us to enrich both the expression and the experience, and at the same time redress whatever balance has been lost.

1. Is the 'foot washing' capable of summing up and presenting the whole of what Christ's ministry and death (together with the return to the Father which is implied) means for man? Does the 'breaking of bread' do this more effectively?

2. Does either one contain what the other lacks? Has the church lost something of the gospel by exclusive sacramental concentration on the breaking of bread, with the foot washing left as an optional ceremony on Maundy Thursday?

(c) *Jn 13:21–30. Judas and the beloved disciple*

The scene of the last supper continues with this short episode in which the mounting tension caused by the presence of Judas is depicted. It starts with our being told that Jesus was deeply troubled. We have seen this said of him several times before, twice in the Lazarus incident (11:33 & 38) and once in the Johannine 'Garden of Gethsemane' prayer (12:27). In each case it is when he is confronted with the power of Satan and, as it were, does battle against him. It is the same here.

In this scene for the first time we have mention of the 'beloved disciple'. He is depicted as resting in Jesus' bosom just as Jesus does in relation to his Father. The beloved disciple is in effect the ideal christian, and here stands for the perfect disciple in contrast to the diabolic one. He thus makes his first explicit appearance at a suitable moment (with typical Johannine sense of drama). Nevertheless he is clearly not simply a symbol but very much a disciple of flesh and blood (cf 13:23–25, in which there is nothing symbolic. His probable identity has been discussed in the introduction, and does not really concern us again here.)

In 'dipping a morsel' and handing it to Judas (13:26) it is quite likely that Jesus was doing him an extreme honour, and we can see how the fullness of Jesus' love and concern is what makes Judas finally and irrevocably bring upon himself the full judgment which its rejection implies; and thus: 'Satan entered into him' (13:27), and Jesus dismisses him to do his worst. This is the hour of darkness when Satan is fully at large, and we recall Jesus' words:

'Night is coming, when no one can work' (Jn 9:4).
'If any one walks in the night, he stumbles,
  because the light is not in him' (Jn 11:10).

Judas has preferred darkness to light, and the hour of darkness has come.

Is the dichotomy between receiving and rejecting Jesus as stark as John seems to depict it? If so, what about us?

(ii) Jn 13:31–14:31. The farewell speech

(a) Jn 13:31–38. Introduction

The original account of the last supper finished off with this farewell speech. Its stylistic genre is of considerable antiquity, and as a literary form it was very popular. Deuteronomy, for example, contains a number of 'farewell speeches' from Moses to the Israelites, and there

are many other examples throughout the old testament;
many of them are pure literary invention, some of them
may well have been based on traditional material going
back way before their literary formulation. Naturally
the speech tends to take the form of a summary and
survey of the situation at which one has arrived, which is
then followed by comments on the future prospects of
those who have been left behind; a father's death bed,
with his family around him, is a typical setting for such a
speech. The situation here in the gospel is obviously
analogous.

The introductory section of the speech (13:31–38) is
given its impetus by the departure of Judas. The hour of
glorification has come, Jesus is returning to the Father
and thus leaving his disciples. They will not, however,
be left destitute and without identity, because if they
keep his 'new commandment' (13:34) they will remain,
and be seen to be, his disciples still. This theme is going
to be developed considerably in several ways; but its
immediate effect is to produce Peter's protestation (13:
37). Characteristically of the fourth gospel Jesus' answer
indicates that Peter has missed the point (again); he
wants to be the perfect disciple and lay down his life for
Jesus. The answer in effect indicates that this is not
possible; Peter can only lay down his life effectively by
following Jesus, because Jesus himself has to go through
death in order to lead his disciples into life. Peter is going
to have to learn this the hardest way.

One can see that this section is a mixture of traditional
elements and specifically Johannine themes. The Johannine themes, however, dominate; comparison of the
account of Peter's predicted betrayal with those in the
synoptics shows the particularly Johannine slant. There
is also a hint here of eucharistic terminology: 'I am

giving you a new commandment' (13:34) would seem to have more than merely accidental affinities with Luke's: 'The new covenant in my blood' (Lk 22:20); and this gives a hint as to how John's phrase is to be understood: once again Jesus is indicating the way in which the old order is being transformed into one centred personally on himself.

But a number of problems remain here. How is the commandment to love a 'new commandment'? How does it compare with or differ from anything in the synoptic tradition? The differences are certainly noticeable. The disciples are being told to love *one another*, not simply to love their neighbours. It is in fact an exclusive instruction on Jesus' part, and has a certain similarity with ideas to be found within the Qumran community. The point is that in loving one another they embody, in their inter-relationships, the spirit of Christ, and thus, as we will see, have his presence truly among them. The idea here is of the christian community being, through its mutual love which is also Christ's love, the embodiment of his continued presence amongst men. Ultimately it is not an exclusive concept at all because Christ is going to embrace as his disciples all men who will come to him; but it has a certain exclusivity with regard to the immediate handing on of his presence—an exclusivity based on love, it should be noted, rather than on any authoritarian concept.

How do 'love one another' and 'love your neighbour' relate to each other? Their ultimate purpose would seem to be the same; their immediate objective quite different—at least in style. If one practises both, which surely one must, do they simply merge? or are we missing something? Is there any analogy here between 'liberal humanism' and 'revolutionary solidarity'? Can they be reconciled? Can they be christian?

(b) Jn 14:1–14. Seeing the Father

The speech now moves from the introduction into the first of its main sections. A great deal of what we find here is simply a reiteration, with a new context, of ideas which we have already seen. The result is to bring them out in greater clarity, because this new context is not something hovering, mirage like, on the horizon but has became real and close at hand. Among these themes we have prominently here that of the unity of will and of action between Son and Father. Because 'the hour' has now come the presence of the Father is very close: instead of the earlier formula 'I and the Father are one' (10:30) we have here the (for us) more intimate 'He who has seen me has seen the Father' (14:9).

The chapter has started off by indicating that Christ's going away is precisely for the sake of achieving this intimacy between the disciples and the Father. To Thomas' question (14:5) Jesus in effect says: 'You do indeed know where I am going: I am going to the Father; and I am the way to him for you, because I am truth and life.' His answer to Philip is of a similar nature. The apparent alternative offered in 14:11 'or else believe me for the sake of the works themselves' is not so much an alternative as a plea for them to realise that his works have indeed witnessed to his union with the Father, a communion which they are to share. This is clinched with an appeal to faith, for it is by faith in Jesus that this communion is achieved.

Do we see the Father? What can this mean for us? Do we see Christ? How can we see Christ?

(c) Jn 14:15–26. 'Keep my commandments'

Three times in this section we are reminded of the need

to keep Christ's commandments (14:15, 21, 23). This cannot be understood primarily as a call to obedience; its purpose is simply to recall and reiterate the earlier statement: 'I am giving you a new commandment' (13: 34), and indeed the explanation which we gave there of the way in which this 'new commandment' ensures the presence of Christ amongst his disciples is enlarged here and spelled out in different ways. First of all we are told of the paraclete (RSV: 'counsellor', 14:16) whom the Father will send. The material here is sketchy and it may seem difficult to see how this paraclete ensures the presence of Christ rather than replacing him. We can in fact only assert the former by appeal to what is said on this subject in the following chapters. Since the bulk of the material on the paraclete is to be found there (Jn 16, and also Jn 15) we will discuss the whole subject there rather than here.

'I will not leave you orphans' (14:18) ties in with the paraclete theme, but is developed differently in the verses which follow. Jesus will not be absent from them because he and his disciples share life—the life of the Father (14:19–20). He also will not be absent because they share a common love—again in the Father (14:21). These ideas are re-expressed in 14:23–24 after the intervention of Judas (not Iscariot). This intervention in effect points to the way in which, as we have suggested, it is the christian community that primarily presents Jesus to the world, through its embodiment of him in the spirit of love. Throughout all this one can see the way in which the presence of God amongst them is being preached to the early church.

This section ends with another reference to the coming of the paraclete (14:26); and this forms an 'inclusion' with the reference to him at its beginning (14:16), thus binding this section firmly together. At the same time, however, it acts as an introduction to the final stage of the farewell.

What sort of obedience should the church demand of her members, to be true to Christ? What sort of demands might in fact be a betrayal of Christ?

(d) Jn 14:27–31. The peace of Christ

At this point the discourse returns more closely to the actual circumstances in which it is depicted. Jesus is bidding them farewell, encouraging them, and indicating his immediate departure—even ending with the formal closure of the supper scene: 'Rise, let us go hence' (14:31).

To represent what Jesus is saying with the words 'Peace I leave with you' (14:27) is extremely unsatisfactory. *Shalom* is a traditional salutation which means 'greetings' or 'goodbye', 'welcome' or 'farewell'; but its basic meaning is 'peace'. Jesus is using it ambiguously, and then spelling out the ambiguity by saying 'not as the world gives do I give to you' (although this also has a double meaning). It is as if he were saying 'goodbye' (ie God-be-with-you) and then adding 'and I really mean that'. There is also the sense of a bequest here, which fits in well with the literary genre of the speech; the 'presence of God' indicated in the 'goodbye' is what Jesus is leaving them. R. E. Brown has rendered it: 'Peace is my farewell to you.'

The second level of double meaning can be seen here when one considers the prophetic nature of this peace. It goes with life, light and justice amongst men, and is of course an indication of, as well as an intrinsic quality of, the messianic age. Although it goes much further, and thus is not like the peace the world gives (14:27), it is nevertheless a terrible mistake to think that what is being talked about is something totally disconnected from 'worldly peace'. It is something less purely negative, something going much further than it, but not something which is a substitute for it; such 'spiritualisation' of the concept would be utterly alien to the evangelist's mind.

With a farewell blessing such as this, then, Jesus goes out into the night to meet his destiny (14:31b).

What is Christ's peace? How can 'worldly' peace be the denial of it? How can worldly peace go towards its achievement? If it were simply 'peace of soul' would this be a heritage that made Jesus a living reality among us, or not?

[Jn 15:1–17:26 The additional discourses to be found in the gospel at this point are commented on, for the reasons given above (pp 124–5), in the general Conclusion. If anyone should want to consider them at this point rather than then, as recommended, he will find them there in their entirety, pp 178–193.]

Jn 18:1–19:42. The passion

The account of the passion in John occupies two chapters. For the most part throughout the gospel the traditional chapter divisions have coincided well with the natural divisions of the material and we have been able to proceed chapter by chapter. Here however the division is inconvenient, for the passion narrative falls correctly into three parts. They are as follows:

1. Arrest and preliminary interrogation: Jn 18:1–27.
2. Jesus before Pilate: Jn 18:28–19:16.
3. The crucifixion: Jn 19:17–42.

The middle section, Jesus before Pilate, is in fact a highly wrought literary and dramatic composition, and if it is not taken as a whole, this important fact can be missed.

This observation raises the whole question of the inter-relation, in this 'account', of historical accuracy and theological/dramatic presentation. We have seen all along how we should not look for 'narrative accuracy' in the fourth gospel. Nevertheless we have also seen how closely the dramatic and theological construction of the gospel depends upon the material reality on which it is based; and we have also noted the way in which (contrary to the generally accepted, but now collapsing, view) there is a tradition of considerable authority underlying the gospel, which in places may very easily be more accurate than that behind the synoptics.

We now have to bring this knowledge to bear on the passion (and resurrection) 'narratives'; it is easy to forget what we have learned here because of the fact that all the evangelists are describing what would seem at first sight to be a simple and straightforward event. The considerable differences between all four accounts should, however, warn us of what is happening. There have been numerous attempts at harmonising these accounts; but these invariably fail because they basically assume that what we have here is something similar to the different accounts, in four different newspapers, of a single straightforward event.

But what in fact we have is a number of different traditions, originating with eyewitness and hearsay accounts, which then developed theologically within different contexts, became intermixed with one another, and were finally written up and re-written up with different theological perspectives in view. The Johannine tradition is probably simpler in many ways than the tradition behind the synoptics, and thus quite possibly, with regard to some of the problems, more accurate. There is internal evidence in places to support this. At the same time, however, John appears to have certain lacunae, more probably because of lack of knowledge than from any theological consideration.

The Johannine account is nevertheless as much as ever a dramatisation and poetic expression of the occasion—which does not make it any the less a genuine presentation of the actual reality. One should note also that, particularly here, the synoptic accounts tend every bit as much towards a similar style of presentation. Thus attempts at harmonising are normally fundamentally misconceived. What we do have to ask, however, is what relationship there is between primitive tradition and theological and dramatic 'write-up' in the various phases of the story. In the public ministry we have seen how sometimes the 'sign' which is being presented is a straightforward incident, such as the healing of the cripple at the pool of Bethzatha (5:2–18), and sometimes a complex encounter, with dialogue and discourse intermixed, such as the scene with Jesus at the feast of tabernacles (7:1–52). Here in the passion narrative the first and final sections tend, with provisos, towards the first category, whilst the central section, Christ before Pilate, falls clearly into the second. Our approach to the narrative must allow us to see this, and at the same time must take it into account.

(i) Jn 18:1–27. Arrest and preliminary interrogation

In the scene of the arrest (18:1–11) two particular points stand out. The first is that when the soldiers and officers arrive Jesus as it were presents himself (18:4) and declares 'I am he' to their question; they are then presented as falling to the ground as a result. Although

the answer is a straightforward reply to a question, John
is showing that it has further significance; even in this
hour Jesus still confronts the world in his divine majesty;
his surrendering *himself* in this way is a radical part of the
revelation of what he is. The words are purely human:
'I am he', ie Jesus the Nazarene; but their significance,
John is telling us, is 'I am'. The Johannine Jesus is shown
throughout the passion narrative as master of his own
destiny, he himself even forcing the pace. Connected
with this is the way in which Jesus, in surrendering
himself, 'bargains' for the freedom of his disciples (18:8);
he uses his divine power to protect his followers, but not
to prevent his own destiny from being fulfilled.

Jesus is now taken to the house of Annas (18:12–13).
Here we have an interrogation (which does not appear
in the synoptics) prior to a trial by the sanhedrin (which
does not occur in John). Again, although the scene is
probably based on early traditional witness, its presentation is dominated by the same sort of theological interest.
The accounts of Peter's betrayal and Jesus' interrogation
are carefully woven in together, with considerable effect:
we are presented with truth itself, Jesus, standing steadfast before his accusers, whilst by way of contrast man,
represented by Peter, exhibits the depth of infidelity. In
other words the polarisation which we have seen throughout the gospel is here seen at its most stark, not as an
abstraction but as something deeply rooted in a truly
human and tragic situation.

*Is there any fundamental difference between Peter's betrayal of
Jesus and Judas'?*

(ii) Jn 18:28–19:16. Jesus before Pilate
In the synoptic gospels the accounts of Jesus before

Pilate are simple and straightforward: Jesus is questioned about his claim to be a king; the crowd demands the release of Barabbas instead of Jesus; under its pressure Pilate hands Jesus over to be crucified. Throughout Jesus is silent. Luke has the bit about Pilate sending Jesus to Herod, and they each include, though in different ways, the mocking of Jesus by the soldiers.

By contrast we have in John one of those highly dramatised and finely wrought constructions which we have already seen in the depiction of the public ministry, but this time it reaches its apogee. The scene is split between two levels: the inside room of the praetorium and the outside courtyard. Inside is Jesus, outside are the Jews; inside we have relative calm and reason, outside the hysteria of fanaticism. The action and dialogue take place through the person of Pilate who at the same time bridges the two levels by moving backwards and forwards between them:

Part 1

1. Pilate goes *outside* to meet the Jews; they demand Jesus' death (18:28–32).
2. Pilate goes *inside* the praetorium and interrogates Jesus on the nature of his kingship (18:33–38a).
3. Pilate goes *outside*, says that Jesus is innocent and offers to release him; they demand Barabbas instead (18:38b–40).

Interlude

4. Pilate returns *inside* and has Jesus flogged; the soldiers mock him (19:1–3).

Part 2

5. Pilate goes *outside* again and presents Jesus to them as innocent. They demand his crucifixion by Pilate (19:4–8).

6. Pilate returns *inside* and cross-questions Jesus about the nature of his power (19:9–11).
7. Pilate has gone *outside* to the Jews, wanting to release Jesus. The Jews argue for and obtain his condemnation (19:12–16).

One should notice how the movement of this scene is circular, reflecting back on itself step by step. Compare 1 and 7: the Jews demand and obtain Jesus' death; 2 and 6: Pilate discusses kingship and power; 3 and 5: the Jews accept Barabbas and reject Jesus. But this circular 'inclusion' is not a static one; the action has moved dynamically and irrevocably, and in that movement is its meaning.

This is not the only structure of the scene, however; running concurrently with it is the way in which Pilate becomes more and more convinced of Jesus' innocence whilst the pressure put on him by the Jews becomes greater and greater until they betray themselves completely by saying 'We have no king but Caesar', and Pilate betrays his integrity by handing over Jesus to be crucified.

All that needs to be added to this before we consider the theological implications is that apart from the drama and 'artificiality', together with minor aspects which are unlikely from an historical point of view, the Johannine account of the trial is the most consistent and intelligible of all of them. John makes it clear that Jesus was brought to Pilate on a political charge and shows with clarity the actual way in which Pilate finally succumbed to the mob pressure of the Jews. There would seem here to be elements of a primitive tradition worked up into a theological and dramatic whole.

It is not possible to say that the omission of the trial before the sanhedrin is due to John wanting to put the blame on the 'worldly authorities'; even if Pilate does assume responsibility for the action the villains in this trial are 'the Jews'—the religious authorities. However, the high point, or rather the utter abyss, of their rejection of Jesus, and thus of their 'worldliness' in the Johannine sense, is identified with their submission to the 'worldly authority': 'We have no king but Caesar' (19:15).

Although, if one is not careful, one is in danger of reading into it concerns which are not in the mind of the author, one can nevertheless see here something like a condemnation of the state taking on the neutral role of judge between truth, or rather ultimate truth, and its perversion. The neutrality cannot be maintained and the worldly power is dragged down to the level of mob violence. Pilate claims to have complete power over Jesus (19:10), but ironically it is the Jews who effectively have him in their power; 'Pilate sought to release him, but ... he handed him over to them to be crucified' (19:12 & 16).

This ironic twisting of the position in which one believes oneself to be is indicated here in another way. Throughout the gospel we have been confronted with people who want to stand aloof from judging between light and dark, truth and falsehood: Nicodemus, the Samaritan woman, and now Pilate. People like the first are condemned because 'they have loved the praise of men more than the praise of God' (12:43; this can apply to Pilate too). The second is forced out of her position of neutrality, as a Samaritan, by the power of truth itself confronting her, and so in fact is Pilate; faced by incarnate truth he answers it with mockery: 'What is truth?' (18:38).

For John, however, the real villains are 'the Jews', ie the pharisees (Introduction, pp 12–14). Of course this bears all the signs of the polemics between Jesus and the pharisees which were then carried into the later part of the century by their respective followers. Nevertheless the reason for their condemnation is clear: they were the people, the heirs of Moses himself, who betrayed their heritage, whereas Jesus fulfilled it; they were the people who abused the authority which came to them from God, whereas he lays down his life for his sheep.

Despite the continuous triumph of Christ throughout his final hour the suffering and the humility is not something that John ignores. Pilate's presentation of Jesus, crowned with thorns, with the words 'Here is the man', forms the tragic climax of the scene. We are forced to recall in particular:

> His appearance was so marred,
>   beyond human semblance,
> and his form beyond that of the
>   sons of men. (Is 52:24)

'Behold the man!' And what we behold is the Son of Man —the irony is as Johannine as ever.

Not only is our attention drawn to the suffering servant theme here, but we are once again reminded of the lamb of God, whom John the Baptist proclaimed at the beginning of the ministry. The priests were about to slaughter the lambs for the paschal meal, and thus could not risk defilement by going in to Pilate (18:28); so Pilate came out to them, and there on their 'own territory' they involved themselves in the ultimate defilement: 'Away with him, crucify him ... we have no king but Caesar' (19:15). The rejection of everything they stood for is total. The messiah, the king of Israel, has come; and at the sixth hour on the day of the preparation of the passover (19:14) he is handed over to them to be crucified, to be raised up before all men.

1. What is truth? What are its demands? Has John answered this? If Pilate could not face it, are we any better off?

2. What is the guilt of 'the Jews'? If we try to get out of their position by distinguishing between an 'earthly' kingship and a 'heavenly' kingship, are we really being true to Christ? Is it as simple as this, or if we answer like that are we really behaving like Pilate?

(iii) Jn 19:17–42. The crucifixion

Here in the scene of the crucifixion we find a structural pattern similar to that in the trial scene—what is called a chiastic pattern: a circular step by step return and inclusion. This, however, is as far as the similarity goes. In the trial this pattern gave it its dramatic strength and movement: here its role is almost entirely symbolic, for the real action is over. There are five episodes with an introduction and conclusion. The introduction and the conclusion indicate the nature of the whole scene (or one might even accurately call it tableau): for John the crucifixion is a royal enthronement, the messiah is lifted up and glorified. This is briefly indicated without elaboration, except that Jesus is shown, as always in John, as being his own master carrying the cross himself (19:17–18). The conclusion (19:38–42) consists of the burial of Jesus. The story is almost identical in all four gospels, with one major exception: John mentions the body being anointed (with a fantastic quantity of spices) before the burial. In other words the scene is presented as a royal burial. Jesus throughout is king, his kingship having come to its fulfilment.

Now we will consider the episodes one by one, indicating their symbolic references. (It is left to the reader himself to trace the connections which constitute the chiastic pattern spoken of above.)

Jn 19:19–22. The Jews have rejected their messiah king; it remains for a gentile to promulgate it to the whole world in 'all the languages' of the world.

Jn 19:23–24. The seamless robe is a priestly symbol, something sacred. The messiah has come as a priest as well as a king, he offers his life for others and consecrates his death for mankind. Note that there are similarities between the theology of the epistle to the Hebrews, which is specifically concerned with Christ's priesthood, and that of John, particularly with regard to Christ's death and resurrection.

Jn 19:25–27. Jesus' mother was told at Cana that his hour had not yet come; she had no role in his ministry. Now the hour has come and she is once more a mother— the mother of all christians, represented here by the beloved disciple. Jesus' concern for the future of his followers is expressed here; it is spelled out fully in the final discourse. (For a most interesting speculation on the possible relationship between John the son of Zebedee = beloved disciple?, which is in no way fanciful, see R. E. Brown, op cit pp 904–906.)

Jn 19:28–30. Here we have various themes of fulfilment. Jesus' suffering is brought to its climax in his cry 'I thirst'. But John depicts him as conscious of the significance of it all to the end. No particular scripture seems to be referred to here, but rather that the whole life leading to death is in fulfilment of the scriptures. The other phrase, 'It is finished', meaning also 'This is the fulfilment', refers to the work he has achieved—his Father's will. Finally the giving up of the spirit has unusual wording (compared with the synoptics). It would be better rendered as 'He handed over, or handed on, his spirit'. The reference is undoubtedly to the way in which the gift of the Spirit to his disciples is concurrent with his

return to the Father. This is spelled out and dramatically represented during and after the resurrection
appearances; here it is pointed to with simple economy.
Jn 19 : 31–37. This episode takes place after Jesus' death.
It thus represents the 'time of the church'. The outpouring of the Holy Spirit which is so essential to the life
of the church is again represented. Most noticeably
recalled is the saying: 'Out of his heart will flow rivers
of living waters' which we are told was said about the
gift of the Spirit (7 : 38). Its sacramental life is vital to the
church, being also that through which Christ's presence
to his disciples continues to be a reality. Thus it is not
surprising to find here a secondary symbolism belonging
to both baptism and the eucharist. (For comment on
19 : 35 see below, pp 174–5.)

This completes the scene, or rather the tableau—for
tableau is exactly what it is. The similarity of structure
between the trial scene and the crucifixion is so strong
that the differences between them stand out all the more
starkly. The trial is a dynamic depiction of a struggle in
action which ends on a climax of betrayal and tragedy;
its very dynamism is indicated, and conveyed, by the
circular yet forward-moving structure with its dramatic
linkage. The crucifixion has a similar structure, but the
linkage is one of ideas rather than dramatic, and the
circularity is almost static; it is as if the final scene in a
play were a photographic still projected onto a screen.
It depicts the eternal implications of what has happened,
much in the same way as an early Italian renaissance
fresco attempts to capture the 'essence' of a complex
event and express it in a single scene.

*1. If the crucifixion is the death-in-which-death-is-con-
quered, where is the life in this depiction of it?*

2. Christ is lifted up; how can we see all men being drawn to him in this? If the picture here is 'static', does John give us the 'dynamism' anywhere? and, if so, how is it related to this 'still'? In what way do we have to wait for the resurrection?

Jn 20 : 1–29. The resurrection

We have just seen how, in John, the drama really comes to its climax at the end of the trial when the ultimate polarisation between acceptance and rejection of Jesus is brought about. Everything that follows on from this is depicted in the crucifixion; Christ is as much alive as dead, or in a sense very much more alive than ever; he is king ruling over the world and mankind from the throne which is precisely the death-which-itself-ends-death. He has been lifted up; on the cross he is glorified; he has in fact gone back to his Father, and we who are his disciples now live with the Spirit which he and the Father give to us. The work is completed, there would seem to be no more to say.

In complete contrast with this the synoptic depiction of the scene presents us with drama right the way through to the death on the cross and beyond. In John the 'high point' of tragedy has been reached with Pilate's presentation of Jesus to the Jews with the words 'Behold the man!' (19:5); the same point is reached in the synoptics with Jesus' death on the cross. The drama is however clearly not finished, it needs the resurrection to complete it.

To summarise this we can say that in the synoptic theology (generally speaking and extremely simplified) the drama of the life and death of Jesus is completed and given its full dimensions by his being raised up again by the Father on the third day. This theology is continued in a series of post-resurrectional appearances, which end with an ascension into heaven, and which is then followed by the outpouring of the Holy Spirit on the church.

The Johannine theology, as we can see from the whole gospel up to now, is different. The crucifixion is the return of the Son to the Father, and as a result his glorification. It is the ultimate expression of the union between Father and Son which has existed from all time. What has been achieved is that all men are drawn to him in his glorification. Heaven and earth are joined, and those who believe in him are taken into his glory, into the love between Father and Son. The ideas of the resurrection and the ascension are contained here, but contained in such a way as not to need temporal or historical expression. This is not to say that they are abstractions, for they are totally integrated with the human life which Jesus shared with his disciples whilst living amongst them, God as true man.

These differences must now be taken fully into account as we turn to the presentation of the resurrection in this gospel. If we try to judge what is presented to us here in terms of the synoptic theological perspectives—and it is extremely difficult for us to avoid this—we will inevitably misunderstand what John is saying.

(i) Jn 20:1–18. The first appearance

(a) Jn 20:1–13. The empty tomb

In the first half of this chapter we can see, by comparison with the synoptic accounts, that a certain number of primitive traditions with regard to the resurrection have been combined, abridged, developed, and finally made the vehicle for dramatic representation of the theological insights of the author.

The traditional stories can be summarised as follows:

first, there is an account of the way in which a number of women followers of Jesus came to the tomb on the Sunday morning and reported to the apostles that they had found it empty. This story appears in John, possibly split up or possibly in two different versions, in 20:1–2 and 20:11–13. Characteristically the people involved have been reduced for dramatic purposes to one principal: Mary Magdalene. The angels in the tomb would have been introduced in the first place by way of inter- pretation; in John, however, this is displaced by the story of the apostles at the tomb and the bit about the angels now stands as introduction to Mary's encounter with Jesus.

The account of the apostles going to have a look for themselves constitutes the second piece of primitive material; obviously the role played by the 'beloved disciple' is 'theological' and we will return to it shortly. The third story is that of Jesus appearing first of all to Mary Magdalene (cf Mk 16:9; originally in company with other women? cf Mt 28:9); it has probably come down in several different forms and been incorporated in the synoptic gospels rather late, which does not necessarily indicate anything about its origin. In John it is given very notable attention, and his handling of it is of considerable theological significance; we will thus treat it as a separate incident.

In the original form of the story the disciples having gone to the tomb and found it empty went away puzzled (Lk 24:24; see also 24:12—a redactor's addition of traditional material rather than a scribal gloss); they had to wait for Jesus' appearances to them before they could understand. Here, however, we have Peter accom- panied by the beloved disciple in a way which is particu- larly stressed, and the story has a very different ending.

Contrary to what many theologians have maintained, it is not really possible to find any indications of a primacy allotted to Peter in this incident, nor on the other hand of an early struggle between Petrine and rival claims. Peter is neither particularly honoured nor is he denigrated, though the 'hero' is undoubtedly the beloved disciple—he is, after all, the hero of this whole gospel, and is generally depicted as a friend and companion of Peter (even when there is no theological influence at work). The primary point being emphasised here is that it is his love that reveals to him what has happened. He comes to realise the implications of the empty tomb because the mutual love between him and Jesus, which derives from Jesus and on which the most profound understanding of him rests, gave him an insight into what it has been all about. Of course the tomb had to be empty, for Jesus had returned to his Father in being lifted up.

Here, in effect, in the form of one dazzling insight, we are dramatically presented with the realisation which came to the evangelist throughout the whole process of the development of the thought of the fourth gospel. We are given a hint of this in the parenthetical verse which follows: 'As yet they did not know the scripture. . . ' (20:9).

Whose tomb was empty? Christ's? the apostles'? ours? How do these effectively link up together?

(b) Jn 20:11–18. Jesus and Mary Magdalene

Now for the first time in John we have a post-resurrectional appearance. That such appearances had a powerful effect on the church's original understanding of the gospel is indicated by the stress laid upon them in

1 Cor 15:5. But it would seem that fairly shortly· this emphasis was to be replaced by the realisation that the entire history of Israel, seen as fulfilled in Christ, implied that the death of Jesus was in fact not death but the conquest of death: '"Was it not necessary that the Christ should suffer and enter into his glory?" and beginning at Moses and all the prophets, he interpreted to them in all the scriptures the things concerning himself' (Lk 24:26–27). And possibly as the result of this sort of awareness the post-resurrectional appearances in the synoptic gospels show a considerable lack of consistency and even of particular concern.

In John the appearances are in no way represented as 'proofs' of the resurrection, they are used as dramatic presentations of its theological implications—or rather of the theological implications of Jesus' glorification. The *raison d'être* of such presentation is in fact to respect the original tradition and at the same time to link it and the theological implications together. The theological and cultural perspectives of Luke enable him to present the overall reality in terms of death followed by resurrection, followed by an ascension, followed by the descent of the Holy Spirit on the church. And we should not forget that this presentation is not simple narrative; it is a theological and dramatic presentation as well.

John's perspectives make him take an altogether different line. The ascension and the gift of the Holy Spirit to the church derive directly from the glorification of Jesus on the cross. These have to be spelled out dramatically in such a way as to show their radical connection with the human Jesus who had lived intimately in company with his disciples; or in other words they have to be presented in such a way that they do not become mere theological abstractions.

This is what is happening in the scene between Jesus and Mary Magdalene. Considerable confusion in our understanding of this has been caused not only by our failure to recognise Johannine categories and distinguish them adequately from those of Luke, but also by mis-translations and false estimation of emphasis. The traditional translation of Jesus' words to Mary has been 'Do not touch me', and the emphasis has been seen as being precisely on these words. There is in fact no connection of thought between this incident and that which shows Thomas confronted with the resurrected Christ (20:27); the emphasis is in fact on: 'I have not yet ascended to the Father' (20:17). The message to be given to the brethren is that 'I am ascending to my Father and your Father' (20:18). The whole import of the scene is that the real presence of Jesus to his disciples after his death depends upon his having returned to his Father.

1. How are those who believe in him related to the Father through Jesus' return to him?

2. Is this 'return' something which can be seen as a reality in the life of the church as we know it today?

(ii) Jn 20:19–29. The second appearance

(a) Jn 20:19–23. The gift of the Holy Spirit

Whereas in the first half of this chapter (20:1–18) three original stories seem to have been brought together to form the material with which John makes two major points, here in the second half (20:19–29) we have one story, the appearance of Jesus to the eleven, which has been expanded and rearranged also to make two major points. We are presented with an entirely different picture here from that of the first half of the chapter. The message of Mary Magdalene and the belief expressed by the beloved disciple seem to have affected the group gathered together here in no way at all. This is simply another indication of the way in which John is making use of traditional material not to construct a consecutive narrative but to present the inner and ultimate meaning of the situation—though not in any abstract way, for the primary concern of this scene is with the life of the church, made a reality through the gift of the Spirit.

Certain points need to be made with regard to the setting of the scene before we can consider its overall meaning. First of all one should notice that there is no emphasis here on the physical or spiritual qualities of the risen body. Both these emphases occur in the second half of this section which is its further development. Secondly the greeting 'Peace be with you' (20:19) is no simple salutation. First of all it has to be linked up with the 'farewell gift' at the end of the last supper (see above on 14:27–31); this is the 'real thing', promised there but now made manifest. The same formula is used in the old testament in the context of divine manifestations (cf eg 'Peace be to you; do not fear, you shall not die' Jg 6:23); and there can be no doubt that what we have here is in effect such a manifestation. (Hence probably the joy of the disciples, 20:20, though this may be a further interpretation of a perfectly natural reaction.) Finally one has to realise that at this stage in the scene the showing of Jesus' hands and side probably has no further signification than that of showing the continuity between the crucified and the resurrected Jesus.

Within this setting the scene now moves forward in three distinct but carefully related steps:

1. 'As the Father has sent me,
    even so I send you.' (Jn 20:21)

2. 'Receive the Holy Spirit.' (Jn 20:22)
3. 'If you forgive the sins of any,
      they are forgiven;
   If you retain the sins of any,
      they are retained.' (Jn 20:23).

Up to now in the fourth gospel the twelve, more frequently referred to simply as disciples, have never been
called apostles. Now, however, they receive this title; they
are being sent forth in Christ's name. The typically
Johannine contribution is to show that this sending is
similar to, and of course dependent upon, the way in
which the Son has been sent by the Father. Naturally
they are sent with the Spirit. The scene recalls, not only
in itself but in the actual words used, the breathing of
life into man in his original creation (Gen 2:7); that was
the old creation, this is the new creation. (Consider the
symbolism of breathing on the child in the old baptismal
rite.)

These two ideas of being sent forth and being given the
Spirit are very closely related; the work that the disciples are sent to perform, which is to make known that
'Jesus is the Christ, the Son of God' so that men may
believe and 'have life in his name' (20:31), is the work
that the Spirit performs through them. The connection
is equally there in the Lucan account of Pentecost. One
should not see these two accounts of the bestowal of the
Spirit, which are superficially so different, as in any way
in opposition to one another; nor for that matter should
one see one as being in any way more 'accurate' than the
other. Luke may be preserving the memory of the first
major charismatic expression of the Spirit's presence in
the church, and writing up his theology around this;
John would seem equally to be writing up his theology
around the traditional material available to him, which

may easily be as primitive and authentic as that available to Luke. As Brown (op cit) has put it: the author of neither work was aware of, or making allowance for, the other's approach to the question.

The final saying about the forgiveness of sins must be seen in the context both of the sending of the apostles and of the gift of the Spirit. As we have just said these two together give the living context in which Christ's work (the work he performs for the Father) is extended and promulgated throughout the world. We have seen all through the gospel how this work is to bring salvation to men through bringing judgment to them. This judgment becomes their own self-judgment, for being confronted by Christ they are forced to choose their salvation or condemnation themselves. Christ divides the world for or against him. Now the most striking old testament imagery connected with this saying about forgiving and retaining sins comes from a context in which the prerogatives of kingship are being handed over: 'And I will place on his shoulder the key of the house of David; he shall open and none shall shut; he shall shut and none shall open' (Is 22:22). Thus in the extension of the messianic work of Jesus in the life of the church, those who act with the spirit which he bestows bring his judgment to bear on men in such a way as to make them believe in him or reject him. In other words Jesus is saying: 'Continue my work.'

One should notice the likely connection with Mt 16:19 and 18:18 which talks about binding and loosing in similar terms. Whether these are interconnected or derived independently from a common source, it is impossible to say; the comparison does not, however, really seem to help in any way. Naturally these two texts have been used respectively in support of the theology of the church's *magisterium* and the theology of her confessional practice, but what we should be particularly aware of is the danger of reading pre- and post-suppositions into the text (*eisegesis*) rather than reading from it (*exegesis*). This is not to suggest that the present text is not relevant to such a theology, but it cannot be taken as a simple warrant for a particular practice; its import is far wider than this.

1. Is John in any way stressing the materiality of the risen Christ? Is this truly a human being or an apparition? Does it matter? How seriously do we have to take the physical side of Jesus' resurrection?

2. Are all Christ's disciples, past and present, apostles? Does the church have any special successors to the apostles? Is this a charismatic or institutional role?

3. How can one reconcile the fantastic mercy and understanding of Christ, in confrontation with sinners, with the way in which he seems to force people into a position of accepting or rejecting him? Where, if at all, does the sacrament of forgiveness relate to this?

(b) Jn 20:24–29. 'My Lord and my God'

Now the scene shifts slightly and develops; something different is being presented. The initial (implied) doubt of the disciples upon the appearance of Jesus was resolved by their seeing his hands and his side (20:20). We have already commented on that, but now the evangelist takes up this theme and develops it to say something which he believes to be of great importance. Possibly because of some tradition about his attitude and behaviour (cf 11:16) Thomas is picked to play principal in this scene. It must be pointed out that, although we have the necessary linkage (20:24–25) which prepares the way for what is to follow and at the same time keeps the dramatic action in movement, what follows is not meant to be a straightforward continuation of a narrative. Theologians who, for example, have suggested that Jesus must have given the Spirit to Thomas privately afterwards have simply missed the point at a whole series of different levels simultaneously.

Thomas refuses to believe until he has seen the miraculous proof of Jesus' resurrection. That it is this aspect of the situation that is being emphasised is evident from the way in which his 'lines' (20:25) echo Jesus' earlier condemnation: 'Unless you see signs and wonders you will not believe' (4:48). Jesus does not so much offer him the evidence which he wants as confront him with a challenge: he 'dares him'. At this Thomas collapses, seeing through his own obtuseness; the confrontation by Jesus has brought Thomas to full belief. He now sees through and beyond the miraculous to the essence of what it is all about. In his declaration of belief—the culminating point of the whole gospel—the fullness of the message is summed up. Jesus is Lord, but not only this. 'I and the Father are one' he has said, and in his glorification this is now manifest. Thomas says 'My Lord and my God' (20:28) and thus speaks on behalf of the church, expressing her belief in what the life and death of Jesus means to her—the new covenant between God and man.

The prophet Hosea describes the fulfilment of this new covenant thus:

> And I will say to Not-my-people,
>   'You are my people'.
> And he shall say, 'Thou art my
>   God.' (Hos 2:23)

This 'formula' has been combined with the baptismal

'Jesus is Lord' to express, through the mouth of Thomas, the completion of the covenant and the faith of the church. This faith is embodied in those who have seen, have lived with, touched and handled the Lord (cf 1 Jn 1:1—no reference to Jn 20:27). Through them it is passed on to those 'who have not seen and yet [will] believe' (20:30).

Do the church's failures in any way make faith in her easier? What could we expect a fully successful church to be like? Would a triumphantly successful and faithful church present Christ to men better? And yet the church's failures are a betrayal of Christ; is there not some sort of an enigma here?

Jn 20:30–31. Conclusion

The two verses which follow the scene of Thomas' proclamation are the conclusion to the original gospel. (Ch 21 is an addition.) This conclusion evaluates, not the work of Christ, but what has been written about him. The assertion of 20:30 is not so much that there are many things that John has left out as that what Jesus has done is inexhaustible; to interpret this simply quantitatively would be to indicate that one had misunderstood the whole style, and indeed purpose, of what has been written!

The last words of this conclusion: 'that you may believe that Jesus is the Christ, the Son of God, and that believing you may have life in his name' (20:31) sum up, with incredible finesse, the whole of the Johannine theology which we have seen expressing itself throughout the gospel. Jesus is indeed the Christ—ie the expected redeemer messiah. But he is this because he comes from the Father and is one with the Father; and it is precisely through this relationship that we, if we believe, have life.

4

The epilogue
Jn 21:1–25

Style and provenance

It is clear to almost anyone that the last chapter of John is additional. There have been people who have tried to show that once upon a time, before (a supposed) distribution of the text, this section had been fully integrated into the post-resurrectional narrative of chapter 20. Such an attitude, however, misunderstands the nature of the evangelical authorship; it misunderstands the style and purpose of the post-resurrectional appearances in that chapter; and finally it misjudges the message of this final one. There can be no doubt that this is additional material added on to the gospel after its original formulation and after its secondary development.

In the case of the story of the woman taken in adultery (Jn 8:1–11) it was quite clear that this was not Johannine material, but something coming from a totally different source, which had been added some time after the gospel's completion—the passage is missing from some of the most important textual sources. This present chapter is missing in none of these sources; it would seem always to have been part of the gospel as 'published'. But more important still its style and manner of thought are clearly Johannine, although there are many things about it which show that it is not by the same hand as is the bulk of the gospel. The way in which it is simply tacked on to the end of the gospel rather than woven into it would seem to indicate that it is the work of the 'final redactor' (cf pp 7–9 and pp 122–5), but whether this is the same person who inserted the extra discourses into the last supper narrative it is impossible to say. The balance of probability, however, favours this suggestion.

As an addition of the final redactor we would expect its thought to reflect a later phase of development, and this in fact is exactly what we find. There is a distinctively 'ecclesial' flavour to it; this may be summed up in terms of a concern for the way in which the christian community is now embodying and projecting into the future the life and message of Christ. It would also look as if this redactor stood at a point where the idea of canonicity of scripture was becoming important. He shows a marked respect for the original material, being willing to add to it but not to touch it. At the same time whilst adding to it he still invokes one authorship (21:24). We can surmise that he stands at the end of a complex discipleship focused around the figure who was central to the preservation and development of this witness to Jesus.

Although written right at the extreme end of the evangelical period, and showing distinct signs of this, it does not follow that the traditional material upon which this chapter is based is also inevitably late. In fact there are signs that much of it goes back a very long way. It has, however, been subjected to the same sort of development which we have seen taking place throughout the gospel; and this must have taken place within the same overall context. Thus this chapter is to be taken seriously and not treated as a mere appendix. It is even possible that it can help us to get some aspects of the original gospel into the right perspective. It bears a relationship to that gospel not totally dissimilar to the relationship between Acts and Luke, though it is of course in no way a sequel. The combination of similarities and dissimilarities in this comparison lead us to believe that this chapter is more accurately described as an epilogue than as an appendix.

Structure and interpretation of the scene

It might seem at first sight that the structure of this chapter is very straightforward: a post-resurrectional appearance followed by a dialogue in which Peter and the beloved disciple are compared and contrasted. Considerable stylisation and symbolism is obviously involved, but that is all. Apparently it is, however, much more complex than that, and an understanding of its structure is necessary in order to see what is really happening. Once again the scholarly details involved cannot be presented here, they are very considerable; they can be looked up in the appropriate sources indicated in the bibliography. What we will do here is to present the conclusions, and ask the ordinary reader to take it on trust—not as something absolutely certain, but as something reasonably well established. The way in which it helps our understanding of the chapter should become clear as we proceed.

The first half of the chapter (21:1–14) relates to the second (21:15–23) in much the same way as, throughout John, a 'sign' relates to a discourse following it. The first half involves a miraculous catch of fish followed by a meal shared by Jesus and the disciples; the second half is a dialogue between Peter and Jesus which is concluded with two 'prophecies', one about Peter and one about the beloved disciple. The only trouble with this picture is that it is far from clear how these two halves are in fact related; the second part does not seem to connect up with the first except by pure accident.

What apparently has happened is that in the first half two different stories of post-resurrectional appearances have been put together. One can see the jointing with the way in which, with regard both to the fish and the recognition of Jesus by the disciples, the story is awkwardly continuous across it. The second of these stories seems based on the recollection of an appearance of Jesus to the disciples and of a meal that they shared between them which has only echoes in other parts of the new testament (cf Mt 28:10 and 16–20 possibly together with Lk 24:30). Its significance here is primarily eucharistic and we will return to it shortly.

The first part of the incident is based on the story of the appearance that Jesus made 'first to Cephas (Peter)', mentioned in 1 Cor 15:5 and probably referred to in Lk 24:34. It is, however, preserved more completely in Lk 5:1–11 where it is presented as part of the original calling of Peter. Luke has undoubtedly misplaced this incident in his account of it, and the interesting thing is the reason for this: in the tradition which handed it on it had become more associated with Christ's commission to Peter than with his resurrection. It would seem that it was on account of the former association that it was handed on to posterity. Thus Luke's 'misplacing' it is highly reasonable; his account ends up with the commission to Peter: 'Henceforth you will be catching men' (Lk 5:11).

With regard to the second part of the fishing scene, ie the meal which they have together, it looks as if this may well derive from an account of the first post-resurrectional meeting in Galilee which is mentioned in Matthew (28:16–20). This latter also ends with a commission to the apostles, and this may account for its having got inserted here in the material which has come down to the Johannine redactor; though it may be that the two appearances were always closely associated. The inclusion of this second appearance and its having been run together with the account of the miraculous haul of fishes has unfortunately obscured the relationship of this latter to the rest of the chapter. What we are dealing with here is originally the first post-resurrectional appearance (cf 1 Cor 15:5), and in it Christ, who was deserted by everyone and denied by Peter, now confronts Peter alone. In this confrontation (Jn 21:15–19) Peter is restored to the position that he tried to obtain for himself in the last supper (cf commentary on 13:37); and is then commissioned to be shepherd of Christ's flock. It is fascinating to find that a whole series of loose threads which are lying around all over the place in the synoptics come up together here in the fourth gospel and can be tied together.

So far we have considered the import of the traditional material, now we want to consider its implications and significance as it has been written up and presented here in Jn 21. With regard to the fishing expedition we are probably meant to see its lack of success as an indication that without Jesus we are able to do nothing; our very life comes from him. Probably in the original story it was Peter who recognised the Lord, but here, in parallel with Jn 20:1–10, it is the beloved disciple—most likely for the same reason as there. However, Peter again takes the lead.

With regard to the 'miraculous haul' there are three points to detain us. First with regard to the number. The emphasis put by the text on this large number of fish, 153, is the fact that it was a large number. These fish undoubtedly represent the future believers to be brought in by the disciples. The account of the incident in Luke also seems to carry a similar interpretation, but this is more likely to arise from development than from the original material.

There is a certain type of mind which is fascinated by speculation on the 'mystical' significance of numbers, and as a result there have, not surprisingly, been at least 153 different speculations on this number! It is hard to see any of them as other than fanciful, however ingenious they may be; and there is no real evidence that such symbolic forms (as postulated) would have been understandable to the original readers—though of course naturally one could not deny that they might have been. We are not, however, dealing here with apocalypse, however strong the relation between John and Revelation. The most likely reason for the specification of an exact number here would seem to be connected with the claim to eye-witness knowledge of the events (see below).

What is significant is that the word used in Greek for the net not being torn (21:11) is unusual in the context, but is the same one used to depict divisions (schisms) among the disciples on account of Jesus' teaching (Jn 7:43; 9:16; 10:19). It is likely that the unity of the 'church' really is being indicated here. A similar example of word identity is found with regard to the net being *hauled* to the land (21:11) which is the same as *draw* in 'When I am lifted up from the earth, I will draw all men to myself' (12:32). (It is a pity that modernisation of the English should have caused this reference to be lost.)

Obviously the 'recognition element' in the meal that

follows (21:12–13) has been affected by the earlier recognition (21:7) and thus appears here only in truncated
form. Originally there would probably have been a
'recognition' when Jesus takes the bread and gives it to
the disciples as there is in Lk 24:30–31 (which may well,
in its origins, be closely related to this scene). The eucharistic symbolism here is pretty obvious. (Note how the
representation of the eucharist in the early church is often
in terms other than of bread and wine, the fish and bread
mentioned here being a common theme.) There is a
clear connection with the multiplication of loaves and
fishes in Jn 6 and, as we have seen, that was explicitly
interpreted in eucharistic terms some time during the
gospel's development. What we are meant to learn from
this scene is that the eucharist represents the way in
which we share life with the risen Lord in the messianic
banquet.

We have already commented on Peter's rehabilitation
(21:15–19.) It has been suggested that the threefold
affirmation may be a reflection of liturgical practice;
it is certainly naive to assume that it reflects the threefold denial of Peter because the influence may easily be
the other way round. It is, however, deliberately interwoven with the commission given to Peter to shepherd
the flock. This 'commission' certainly reflects the general
one given to all the apostles to pass on the good news and
'take care' of it; but it would also seem to indicate a
particular authoritative commission as well. Christ himself is the good shepherd (10:1–18) and we saw in
commenting on that discourse how closely this is associated with the idea of messianic kingship (cf Ez 34:24).
The shepherd's role would seem to be an exclusive role;
and it is this role that is being transferred to Peter, the
model shepherd. That such transference is possible is

indicated by: 'As the Father has sent me, even so I send you' (20:21); but it is difficult to see how such a role as that of shepherd could be communicated to many. It is also worth noticing that just as it is the role of the good shepherd to lay down his life for his sheep, so has Peter's rehabilitation now allowed him to take on this role. We believe that it is not altogether fanciful to see here an indication of a particular role being given to Peter.

With regard to the claims made in the later church in connection with the further handing on of this role to the successors of Peter, one has to be as careful here as in the case of forgiving and retaining sins (20:23). It has been well said that logical arguments based on the implications of figurative language are to say the least problematic. It is more valuable to ask oneself the question why the Johannine redactor thought it necessary to take up this point and emphasise it after Peter's death (21:19).

1. Did Christ celebrate the eucharist with his disciples after the resurrection? What on earth could this mean?

2. Does being a 'shepherd of souls' necessarily imply being a 'father figure'? Was Jesus in any way a 'father figure'? Is there any place at all for the title 'Father' in the church? Does its use undermine, or even betray, the gospel?

Jn 21:18–23. The death of the apostles

The material which is now added to the scene looks as if it came from another source. Jesus' words about the future role of Peter have provided a convenient point at which to attach a saying about his death. This leads in turn to the words about the beloved disciple's death. The whole thing has been very cleverly constructed, for it is this last point to which the author has been working

all the time; this is the crucial point of his concern. But
is he writing up for himself this whole last episode or is he
working on traditional material, making it a vehicle for
his message? Apart from the fact that, for any Johannine
author who is running true to form, this latter is much
more likely, there is evidence within the text which indicates that he is working with traditional material. The
point is that neither of these 'sayings' really lend themselves at all easily to the interpretation which is being
forced upon them.

The prophecy of Peter's death might at first sight seem
obvious, but in fact it is extremely vague and full of
puzzles, and it is by no means sure that it originally
meant anything about his eventual crucifixion. Some
scholars think, for example, that the stretching out of the
hands is a reference to prayer. Jn 21:18 really does need
19 to explain it, and it is only then that it seems obvious.
This latter verse is interesting evidence, of a very early
date, for the martyrdom of Peter and of its being widely
known.

The saying about the beloved disciple would equally
seem to be traditional (as the author himself insists,
21:23), for if it had just been invented all that would be
necessary would be to point it out. It would seem that
within the community focused on this disciple there was
in fact a tradition that he would not die before the 'return of the Lord'. And yet he has died. The twofold reiteration of the 'If it is my will that he remains until I
come, what is that to you?' (21:22 and 23) used as a rebuttal of the 'tradition' contains a note of hysteria or at
least of crisis. The implications are that the beloved
disciple has died and this has caused a stir in the community. The Johannine author is trying to reassure them
by relating this saying to the whole scene he has built up

around Peter. What he achieves has other effects as well. He very satisfactorily succeeds in relating Peter and the beloved disciple. Peter, following Christ, dies a martyr's death; the author shows that the way in which his master dies (most likely of old age—very old age) is equally the Lord's will. He is shown throughout as a companion of Peter, and yet one who plays a very different role: Peter's role is shepherd, the beloved disciple's is witness (see below) and preaching and insight through love. Despite what many authors have suggested there do not seem to be any signs of rivalry about authority between these two.

A final point with regard to this is that the whole of this dramatic scene indicates that the beloved disciple is no mere symbol, as has been suggested; his death seems to have caused a stir precisely because he is a real person and one who has links going right back to Jesus. The linkage seemed to the community to have been now broken, and the whole of the theology of the redactor is concerned (as we shall see more fully later) with the way in which this link is in fact not broken.

One should note that the list of Peter's companions given at the beginning of this chapter could be seen as favouring the identification of the beloved disciple with John the Apostle (see our introduction); in making use of this evidence one must however be careful for there may be some symbolic artificiality here since these are the same disciples who were mentioned at the very beginning of the gospel in ch 1. There is an obvious 'inclusion' here, but it is difficult to guess its significance.

1. What is the likelihood that John the apostle was the figure central to the development of the Johannine tradition, and the emergence of the fourth gospel?

2. What is the value, in this gospel, of an authentic tradition going back to Christ himself? Can one really detect the presence of such a tradition?

Jn 21:24–25. The witness

The death of the beloved disciple has been justified—Jesus himself was never saying that he would not die (21:21–23). As we have just seen, the author of this chapter is concerned with establishing the link which exists, despite the death of the last apostles, between the church and its founder. In the sections which have been inserted into the final discourse at the last supper (which will be commented on in the conclusion) we are going to see in action the theology which expresses this; here we have a slightly different aspect of the linkage which he is presenting: the beloved disciple is the witness who stands behind the gospel, and who in fact 'wrote it' (21:24).

To understand this we have to turn back to Jn 19:35. There we have, in the context of the highly symbolic water and blood flowing from the pierced side of Jesus, the assertion that there is a true eye-witness behind the account of what is happening. This does not seem to refer to the author, but rather to the beloved disciple who is mentioned as being present in 19:26. Here in Jn 21 the author takes this up and re-writes it (it was certainly written in the first place by a different hand from his, yet by one in the same tradition). His reaffirmation of the eye-witness character of the events may be the expression of a realisation that he stands (as we have already suggested) as it were at the watershed when canonicity has become important; he is on the one hand declaring that the original work, together with what has been

added, is an authentic witness to Christ, and on the other
he is defying anyone else to alter it further.

There is however another point to be noted. In writing up 19:35 he has in fact added one very significant
point. He has made the claim that it is the beloved
disciple who has '*written* these things' (21:24). Now this
would seem to be obviously untrue. People have tried
to get away from this by pointing out that the whole
concept of authorship at that time is different from our
concept of it. This is undoubtedly so, but hardly seems
to be sufficient. The point that the redactor is making is
that the witness of the beloved disciple has not only been
a living witness during his life time, but that now, after
his death, that witness continues because it is here *written
down.* Thus here we have a very tangible link with
Jesus; it has not vanished with the last of the apostles,
it continues in the new scriptures of the new covenant.
We can thus see that this conclusion (21:24–25), understood in this way, is not just a conclusion tacked on to
the end, but is in fact the conclusion which grows organically out of the whole of this chapter.

We can now make a very interesting comparison between Jn 21 and Jn 20. They are both 'accounts' of post-
resurrectional appearances of Jesus, yet these have distinctively different messages. In many ways, of course,
they are closely connected; they both belong to the same
theological tradition. It is the differences, however,
that concern us. In Jn 20, although there are other
aspects of importance, the resurrected Christ stands primarily as witness to the fact that in his death on the cross
Jesus has been glorified and is once more fully restored to
the bosom of the Father giving life to all who believe in
him. There is a sense in which all is complete; everything
is contained in the triumphant glory.

In Jn 21 the resurrected Christ stands more for the way in which his life-giving power will go forth into the world (though this idea is not absent from 20:21 and 23), and although he is himself in every ordinary sense absent and all human links with him have perished, nevertheless those links remain. There is not so much a sense of 'having arrived' here, as one of 'travelling hopefully'. The 'realised eschatology' of the fourth gospel (which we have nevertheless seen as being tempered again and again) is once more tempered here.

What has become obvious is the great richness of the Johannine tradition—a tradition developed and centred around one who was especially loved by Jesus. Were it all to be written out in full 'I suppose that even the world itself could not contain the books that would be written' (Jn 21:25).

How does the written word stand in relation to tradition in the way the church hands on to men the message of Christ? Is scripture in any way subordinate to the church, or vice versa?

5

Conclusion
Jn 15:1–17:26 and 1:1–18

Comment on the material presented here

Under the heading of 'conclusion' we are presenting not only the prologue but also the farewell speeches which were added by the redactor to the original discourse which terminated the last supper. As we argued in the first chapter of this commentary, the prologue is in fact a conclusion which has been placed at the beginning of the gospel to form an introduction telling us what the gospel is all about. We shall therefore present the prologue as the gospel's own conclusion to itself.

Before this, however, we will look at the farewell speeches. These cannot be regarded as a genuine part of the conclusion in anything like the same way. Nevertheless these speeches were composed from outside the actual gospel narrative and arranged so as to fit into the context chosen for them. They thus reflect both a concern for the significance of the scene depicted—the last supper—and the theological preoccupations of the (late) period at which they were added; this latter is something which we have already seen in the epilogue. These additional speeches do, as a result, take a look at Christ's life and death from a vantage point which is in a way less directly involved in it than were the original evangelist and the later evangelical editors. In this sense they do in fact have some of the qualities which are found in straightforward conclusions; they are thus not out of place if they are presented as an introduction to this section.

Jn 15:1–17:26. The farewell speeches

There are four separate discourses here. The first three together form a unit, and are concerned with the condition of the disciples after Jesus' death; the last is a prayer in which Jesus consecrates his disciples to God. The first discourse is about the true vine; the second about the hostility of the world to Jesus' disciples; the third is about the sending of the paraclete. In our treatment of this latter we will gather together threads which are also to be found in Jn 14 and 15.

(i) Jn 15:1–16:33. The disciples after Jesus' death

(a) *Jn 15:1–17. The true vine*

With this beautiful simile Jesus relates himself to his disciples; he is the vine, of which we are the branches, and his Father is the gardener who looks after it. The seventeen verses of which it is composed clearly form a unity, but within it are two very disparate sections. In the first (15:1–6) the simile is developed in a language devoted entirely to the interrelationships of vine, branches and the gardener, and the explanation of what they denote. These relationships are all presented as actually existing, and there are no signs at all of the circumstances of Christ's final hour, or in other words of any of the characteristic concerns of a farewell discourse. From 15:7 onward, however, these themes come in with a rush and entirely dominate the discourse.

What we have here is the simile, and its immediate development, followed by a sort of commentary on it which encourages and exhorts those to whom it is addressed. Of course 'simile' is not the right word for this, nor is 'parable', nor 'allegory'. It is something looser and more flexible than these, and one can be seriously misled by trying to apply the imagery too rigorously. In fact it never remains on a single plane, but the reality which the symbolism represents keeps breaking through into its description. It is possible that behind this there was an original simile which at some later date had the first explanation which was attached to it fused into it and combined with it. At any rate it obviously comes from a different original context and has been introduced here on behalf of the 'commentary' (its 'second explanation') which is so very relevant to the theme of Jesus' departure. Nevertheless it also fits into this context as an expression of the unity between Jesus and his disciples in the care of his Father. In some sense it can thus be seen as expressing (though only partly) the reality behind the drama; but if we say this we must avoid the danger of seeing the drama and the reality as separate—there is no dualism of this sort in the evangelist's thinking.

The exhortatory commentary has a very careful literary structure turning back upon itself step by step, thus forming a rounded whole in which the ending: 'This I command you, to love one another' is brought into comparison with the way in which Jesus' words have to remain amongst us, mentioned at the beginning. The themes referred to throughout have come up again and again; they mainly concern the fullness of the way in which we are related to the Father as the result of Jesus' relation to him and of ours to Jesus. A slightly new note, however, is introduced by the exhortation 'Keep my commandments, just as I have kept my Father's commandments' (15:10). This is followed later (15:14) by our being told that we are his friends if we do what he commands. That this is not meant in what we would think of as an authoritarian way is clearly indicated by the verse which tells us that we are not servants but rather his intimates (15:15). We are clearly meant to take all this in the spirit of the 'new commandment' discussed earlier (13:34) which is here referred to again in an earlier verse: 'Love one another, as I have loved you' (15:12). What is in effect being stressed is the necessity of a union of love and will between christian and christian, between christian and Christ, such as there is between him and his Father.

Many people have speculated on the origin of this imagery of the vine; whether it is Hebraic or pagan. There is certainly considerable use of vineyard and vine imagery in the old testament, most noticeably in Isaiah (5:1–7) and in Ps 80. This imagery is, however, always associated with Israel (and the sinful and erring Israel at that), whereas John identifies Jesus himself with the vine. But this should not surprise us as it represents a tendency throughout John's thought: where the synoptics have 'The kingdom of God is like . . .' John has similar passages starting 'I am . . .'. Jesus himself, in John, represents the kingdom, the new Israel, and in these passages, in which the solidarity of Jesus and his disciples in the love and knowledge of the Father is being stressed, we can see this process reaching its culmination.

The most satisfactory area of tradition in which to look for sources of this imagery is however, not surprisingly, the wisdom literature, especially Sirach. For example, personified wisdom, which we have come across as a motif throughout John, speaks as follows:

Like a vine I caused loveliness to bud,
  and my blossoms became glorious and
    abundant fruit.
  Come to me, you who desire me,
    and eat your fill of my produce.
Those who eat me will hunger for more
  and those who drink me will thirst for me.
Whoever obeys me will not be put to shame,
  and those who work with my help
    will not sin. (Sir 24:17–22)

Of course this is not saying anything like what is said in this discourse, but the imagery is one stage nearer to the way in which it has been developed by John. The reference in the last verse to 'obeying wisdom' (Sir 24:22) may, also, not be totally disconnected from the way in which John talks about keeping Christ's commandments (Jn 15:10, 12 and 14).

Considerable pagan elements have been combined with Hebraic thought to form the wisdom literature, and therefore it is not surprising that scholars should have found traces of it in John. It would seem, however, that the influence on him is from contemporary judaic thought in the same genre as the wisdom literature, rather than direct from pagan sources.

A final question to be asked is whether there is any eucharistic imagery (in the narrower sense of this) in this simile and its development. As Christ is the living water (Jn 3) and the bread of life (Jn 6) so also he is the true (ie the life-giving) vine. In ch 3 we saw that there were secondary baptismal references, and in ch 6, apart from the specifically eucharistic additional material, there were also secondary sacramental references; is it possible then that here also there is reference to the eucharist?

This would be very difficult to answer if it were not for a considerable similarity of language and ideas between this passage on the vine and the specifically eucharistic section of the bread of life discourse (6: 51–58). Compare, for example: 'Abide in me, and I in you … he who abides in me and I in him' (15:4, 5) with 'He who eats my flesh and drinks my blood abides in me, and I in him' (6:56); compare the way that the health of the vine depends on the Father, and the health of the disciples depends upon their being part of the vine (15:2, 4) and 'I live because of the Father, so he who eats me will live because of me' (6:57). And many more similarities can be detected. It would seem most probable that there is at least some significant secondary eucharistic symbolism here in the discourse as it stands, but in an earlier stage of its history this might have been stronger.

1. How much does unity in Christ depend upon 'outward' and 'social' unity? Is it something physical or spiritual or both? Can the church genuinely be an institution?

2. Who is in the church and who is not? Must one have explicit faith in Christ to be a member of the church? Is the presentation of Christ's life and work among men a necessary role of the church? Does faith depend upon it?

(b) *Jn 15: 18–16: 4a. The world's hatred*

For the most part in John's gospel the major divisions run concurrently with, or at least not against, the chapter divisions. Here, however, a discourse runs right across the chapter division, ending even in the middle of a 'verse'. The RSV shows the ending correctly and also divides the whole section into two at the point where ch 16 begins. It is, however, easier to understand this discourse if we see it as being in four parts: 15:18–21,

22–25, 26–27 and 16:1–4a. These four sections can be summarised as follows:

1. The world hates you because you belong to me, and it has hated me. What it has done to me, it will do to you. (Jn 15:18–21)
2. If I had not come and manifested myself, they would not have been guilty. (Jn 15:22–25)
3. When the paraclete (RSV: counsellor) comes, he will bear witness on your and my behalf. (Jn 15:26–27)
4. I tell you what will happen to you now so that you will be strengthened and ready for it when it comes. (Jn 16:1–4a)

It is immediately obvious how the first and the last are related together. The final section is expressing what the church is experiencing at the time that the gospel is being written. This is explained, and encouragement is given, by referring it back to the way in which Jesus was in conflict with the authorities. The relationship between him and his disciples, if they are true to him, makes it perfectly clear that they too will suffer in a similar way.

The second section (expressing an idea parallel to that of Jn 6:41) can be seen as a theological aside relating to the first, but not developing the line of thought, though it links up with it again at the end (15:25). It is only the third section which looks out of place. It introduces the subject of the following discourse (16:4b–33) which is all about the paraclete. As we shall see in a moment, however, the paraclete theme is in fact closely tied in with the theme of persecution of Christ's disciples. It follows logically on this present discourse, and the appearance of the theme here can be regarded as anticipatory.

In the first section (15:18–21) we have an extended

expression of a theme which we have already encountered frequently. The presence of Christ amongst men divides them into two camps: those who receive and those who reject him. This is not just a passing phenomenon, but a radical effect of his presence. 'The world' for John represents those who reject Jesus—it was, after all, the worldly authorities who condemned and tried to destroy him, and the same authorities who continue to persecute his disciples. Over against this is the church, or in other words Christ and his disciples—those whom he has chosen (15:19). Again it must be stressed that this distinction is not directly indicating what we would today think of as 'worldly' and 'unworldly', though of course there are interconnections between these two sets of ideas.

What we have called a theological aside (15:22–25) can now be seen to be connected with this first section more directly than was first suggested. Hand in hand with the idea of a radical division between those who accept Jesus and those who reject him is the idea of his presence and confrontation with people as precisely the factor which causes them to bring judgment on themselves. Faced by Jesus, in the fullness of what he stands for, man brings his own judgment upon himself. It is interesting, in the light of later theological speculation and controversy, to see how effectively, by way of dramatic presentation, John here solves the problem of the apparent conflict between divine and human causality, between destiny and free will.

Does persecution of the church always indicate that it is doing God's work? Can the 'world' hate the church with just cause?

(c) *Jn 16 : 4b–33. The paraclete*

The first half of this section deals explicitly with the

future coming of the paraclete; the second half presents what was originally separate material embodying a slightly different theological outlook. These two have been deliberately welded together by the 'evangelist' (whether the final redactor, who is responsible for this whole block of material, Jn 15–17, or someone before him it is impossible to say); and this second theme now has to be interpreted in the light of the first. We will thus start by looking at the whole question of this uniquely Johannine figure: the paraclete.

Paraclete means 'one who is called to one's side' and is basically a legal term. It has often been thought that this is enough to explain its usage here in John; it has thus been translated as 'advocate' (JB and NEB) or 'counsel'. But in fact this meaning only fits in with some of the things said about the paraclete. The paraclete is judge as well as advocate, and he is also teacher (16:8–11; 14:26; 16:13). The concept of advocate may well be contained within the idea of 'paraclete' as used by John, but it is clearly not adequate as a translation, nor does it fully explain what is involved. Similarly the idea of comforter (the old translation) is also to be found in 'paraclete', but the term does not adequately cover its content. 'Counsellor' (RSV) does not fare any better.

If we are to understand what is being talked about we must go to the historical background of the concept. What should be noted is that the paraclete is sent by both Jesus and his Father in Jesus' name after he himself has left (14:26; 15:26; 16:7) and that the paraclete carries on the work which Jesus was doing. There is a sort of tandem relationship between Jesus, who has to leave, and the paraclete, whom he sends to take over and continue his work. There are earlier parallels for this which make the idea a powerful one: consider Moses and

Joshua, Elijah and Elisha, even John the Baptist and Jesus himself at the start of the ministry. And it should be noticed that each of the successors is spoken of as receiving the Spirit, and the paraclete is closely associated with, even identified with (14:26), the Holy Spirit.

The idea of the Spirit present amongst men is thus closely connected with the idea of paraclete. This is to be found in the prophets—in them the Spirit of God is at work amongst men; and of course the apostles are, in a way, the successors of the prophets. Through later Jewish thought the whole concept of the Spirit abroad in the world becomes more complex—it has been noted again and again in the wisdom literature; but from Qumran we have a phrase actually used also here in John: 'the Spirit of Truth', who is shown fighting against darkness in a struggle between heaven and earth (*Testament of Judah* 20:1–5; cf Jn 15:26).

All these ideas which go back into judaic history do not of themselves give us an interpretation of what 'paraclete' means for John, but when they are all added up and related to what he says and to the context within which he says it, then a picture emerges which at least has some definite outlines. This context, as we have seen, is a farewell speech; Jesus is talking about the situation amongst his disciples after he has departed from them. 'I will not leave you orphans' he has said (14:18—the earlier passage from the original farewell speech which is parallel to the material here in Jn 15 and 16). He has to go away, but the paraclete will be there in his stead, repeating, carrying on, what Christ has said and done. He will guide them in the way of all truth (16:13).

The identification of function between Jesus and the paraclete is very noticeable, and the paraclete is des-

cribed as 'another paraclete' (14:16). It would be rash
to conclude that the paraclete is a substitute for Jesus,
but he would certainly seem to be the continued presence
of Jesus, while the latter has in a sense gone. The church,
living with his Spirit, is the continuation of the life of
Christ amongst men. The church, with the paraclete as
its principle of life, is in a sense Christ's bodily presence
continued on earth.

The presence of the Spirit, the paraclete, ensures the
continued jointing together of man's earth and God's
heaven, which has been achieved and cemented in
Christ's ministry, passion, resurrection and ascension.
The outpouring of the Spirit is, from one point of view,
precisely the completion of this 'historical process'—its
ultimate fulfilment, and the expression of its radical
unity; from another point of view it is of course simply a
concomitant of the glorification of Jesus. Having the
paraclete as an integral part of our lives means that we,
Christ's disciples, can continue to witness to his ministry
and salvific work and live with a life which comes from
his Father.

We now turn to the second section of this discourse
(16:16–33). It is presented in direct continuity with the
material on the coming of the paraclete, and even linked
organically to it by the reference back of its opening
words to 16:10. Its original separate identity is indicated
both by its theme and by the way in which it is articulated with passages of dialogue. A great part of the
material here is similar to eschatological utterances in
the synoptics, though it is interwoven fully with typical
Johannine themes. There is also a slight tendency towards elements of a future eschatology: 'The hour is
coming . . . in that hour you will ask in my name . . .'
(16:25, 26).

What it is all about is the return of Jesus 'in a little while' (16:16). One might at first imagine that this is a simple reference to the post-resurrectional appearances but, although this might possibly have been so in the original material, one can see from the present discourse that nothing as simple as this is meant; what is really being talked about is the future presence of Christ amongst his disciples. We have seen that in John there is no account of, or even reference to, an 'actual' ascension; rather it is implicit in the whole idea of the Son's glorification. Thus it would seem that although Jesus returns to his Father he never leaves his disciples (except when they leave him) and is still with them—he never actually leaves them in the way that he does in the Lucan theology.

This presents the Johannine author with the problem of what is meant by this return of Jesus 'in a little while' (16:16–18), and the whole juxtaposition of this material with that on the paraclete, the Holy Spirit, would seem to indicate that the author has realised that this presence of Christ talked about here must be understood in the sense of the church's being possessed by the Holy Spirit. This in fact backs up and gives strength to the interpretation of the nature and role of the paraclete which we have just presented.

1. Can the Holy Spirit be said to be incarnate among men? Does this discourse on the paraclete raise any difficulty with regard to the trinitarian 'definition' of three persons in one nature?

2. In what sense is the Holy Spirit a person? What does 'person' mean to us?

3. Are we normally in any danger of tritheism? In what way is the paraclete distinct from the life-spirit of Jesus himself? Does this sort of question make sense or is it pernicious?

(ii) Jn 17:1–26. The prayer of Christ

The author is continuing to respect his literary genre by adding, at the end of a number of farewell speeches, a prayer such as this. Deuteronomy still provides us with a parallel; after all the 'law-giving' farewell speeches it ends with two canticles, the first of which (Deut 32: 1–43) is addressed to the heavens and the second (Deut 33:2–29) is a blessing over the tribes of Israel. Not only is the pattern in Christ's farewell prayer similar (though the differences are equally interesting), but it too is very nearly a canticle. It is closer to strophic poetry than any of the quasi-poetical discourses, and it is interesting to note that in the final version of the gospel it plays a part in the last supper similar to that described in Mark: 'And when they had sung a hymn they went out to the Mount of Olives' (Mk 14:26).

There are also certain rather striking similarities between this prayer and the prologue. They both have a carefully planned poetic structure, and they both contain explanatory prose comments—though in the prayer there are fewer of them. It is a pity that the Jerusalem Bible, the only common version to print these sections out in 'poetic form', misses both these points. There is also some similarity of style and of ideas between this prayer and the hymn to the incarnation in Phil 2:6–11.

Another new testament interconnection, this time precisely theological, is to be found between this prayer and the epistle to the Hebrews. In the latter Christ is depicted as one standing before the throne of God making intercession for us. The role he is playing here in this prayer is very similar; and it is for this reason that it has traditionally been known as the priestly prayer. It contains, however, no idea of propitiatory sacrifice, even although it has been set in the context of the last supper. The similarity between this prayer and the Lord's prayer should also be noted. The prayer is addressed to the Father; it asks for his name to be glorified (=hallowed); there are many implicit references to his will being done; and Christ prays that we should be kept from the evil one (17:15). These similarities are strong enough to suggest that there is at least common material behind them both even if no direct influence from one to the other.

From the point of view of the way in which it presents its ideas the structure of the prayer is fairly simple. It falls into three parts:

1. A prayer to the Father for glorification (17:1–5).
2. A more complex section concerned with the welfare of the original disciples (17:6–19).
3. A prayer for the later disciples who follow after them, or in other words for the future church (17:20–26).

Further comparison with the canticles in Deuteronomy may or may not be valid from a literary or theological point of view, but it can help us to see an important feature of this prayer. Whereas the 'address to the heavens' is in this case relatively short, the 'prayer for the tribes of Israel', ie the prayer for the disciples (17:6–26), is by comparison considerably extended and consists of two parts: concern for the original disciples, ie the apostolic church; and concern for the future church. Here we can detect most noticeably the preoccupations of the author which were pointed out in connection with Jn 21.

The opening section of the prayer (17:1–5) refers directly to the 'final hour'. This is the point from which the author sees the life of Christ flowing out into his church. This life comes from the life shared by the Father and the Son and is made available to us through the Son's glorification. The Son glorifies the Father by passing on this life to men, and thus it can be said that it is in them that he has been glorified (17:10).

A comment in parenthesis explains that the life which is passed on is to be understood in terms of the knowledge of God (17:3). One should not forget, in appreciating this, that knowledge of God has already been expressed in terms of keeping his commandments (15:10–14; cf 1 Jn 1:3; 4:8; 5:3)—and we have seen how this is not to be understood in an authoritarian sense. 'Obedience' and 'knowledge' are very closely related: the Son knows the Father because he does the Father's will. This theme is at the centre of the last two verses (17:4, 5): Jesus has done the work of his Father on earth and takes this work back to him in his glorification.

The train of thought flows straight on into a comment on those who are going to receive eternal life. They are those to whom Jesus has revealed the name of God (17:6a), that is by showing that it is he himself who bears the title 'I am'; they are those who are faithful (17:6b). Christians are those who know that what Jesus has given them comes from the Father; they believe in him because he has not spoken simply for himself but on behalf of the Father (17:7–8).

Christ now prays for these disciples. We can see how they are in need of his prayer if we articulate its content in simple form. We can also see how the church is recognising in itself the need for this prayer, for it expresses so clearly the conditions of the late apostolic church.

> Although I was in the world
> I do not belong to it.

> I am leaving the world;
>> they are still in it.

> I was there and looked after them;
> I gave them your word;
>> the world hated them.

> They are still there,
> but do not belong to the world.
>> Father, keep them safe from evil.

And as a comment on all of this we have in 17:13 'These things I speak . . . that they may have my joy fulfilled in themselves.'

Here once again we have the dualism of John: the world versus the spirit, this last being represented by 'not belonging to the world'. We have explained earlier how this is not a contrast between matter and the non-material, but between accepting Jesus and rejecting him. 'He was in the world' indicates the way in which he confronted men; he dissociates himself from the resultant condemnation, associating himself with those whom the Father has given him (17:6). The disciples remain in confrontation with the world, bringing his judgment to it, yet they are not on the side of the world, but on Jesus' side. Without his help, and the intervention of the Father, they will however fall, and so he prays his Father to save them from the evil one—not just 'evil', but the personification of it which epitomises this dualism.

This part of the prayer (17:6–19) finishes up with Jesus' consecration of his disciples in truth. Earlier in the gospel we have seen how the Father, who is holy, consecrates his Son and sends him into the world (10:36); here Jesus, who is himself the holy one of God, consecrates his disciples, sending them into the world (17:18,

19). The mission is a holy one, otherwise it would bring false rather than true judgment.

This end to the prayer over the disciples has led straight in to the prayer for the future church (17:20–26); 'I do not pray for these only but also for those who are to believe in me through their word' (17:20). The concern of the author now becomes explicit. We have seen, in reference to Jn 21, how he stands at the dividing line between the apostolic and the post-apostolic periods. His concern is with the way in which the linkage between Christ and his disciples continues beyond this point. Here we see it expressed by Christ praying for the disciples of his disciples in continuity with his prayer for the original twelve. The life which he himself bestows is passed on through the word of his disciples (17:20), and in accepting it they reflect the unity of the Father and the Son which is the source of that life. The prayer he prays for them is that they should have amongst themselves this unity, for then only will they be passing on to the world the presence of God to men; and only in as far as they are doing this will they be participating in the life which is shared by the Father and the Son. If they live with his life, they will have in them the love with which the Father loves the Son (17:26). Thus the importance of the Johannine (1 Jn) exhortation: 'Little children, love one another.'

1. How can the church most truly be 'in the world' and yet at the same time 'not of the world'?

2. How is Christ's presence handed on from disciples to disciples? Is 'apostolic succession' an intrinsic part of this process? What are the priorities between anything like this and 'loving one another'?

Jn 1: 1–18. The prologue

We took a preliminary look at the prologue in the opening chapter of commentary, and the reasons for treating
it here as a conclusion are fully gone into there. There
also we showed its literary structure and the way in which
it had most probably been put together. It was recommended at the time that it could be extremely helpful to
underline the three different strata of the text with
different coloured inks or crayon. This recommendation
is repeated again; not only is it helpful, particularly in
the discussion which follows, but it also produces, if done
neatly, a very pleasing effect.

We are now going to present the prologue again, not
this time according to its literary structure, but according
to the division of its ideas.

1. (a) In the beginning was the word
       The word was with God
       The word was God
              (He was in the beginning with God)
   (b) All things were made through him
       Without him was not anything made that was
           made

2. (a) In him was life
       The life was the light of men
   (b) The light shines in the darkness
       The darkness has not overcome it

3. (a) He was in the world
       The world was made through him
       Yet the world knew him not
   (b) He came to his own home
       His own people received him not
              (But to all who received him . . .)

4.   The word became flesh
       and dwelt among us
              (full of grace and truth . . .)

This is the hymn which has been used to head the gospel;
the theological comments which were added to it at
some stage in its development (cf p 32) are added here
in parentheses. The first of these comments simply
rounds off and completes the opening phrases, as it were
gathering them up and holding them as a beacon above
all that follows; the remaining comments, which grow
in quantity as the prologue proceeds, are indications of
the way in which it is being applied to the ideas expressed
in the original gospel. The question which must be
asked is whether this 'hymn' has come from an extraneous, possibly pagan or possibly purely judaic, source, and
has thus been applied to the gospel as an interpretation of
it, or whether it is something which has developed, along
with the fourth gospel itself, in the Johannine community.

   We have drawn attention to the beacon-like qualities
of the first lines in 1 (a); we can see how 1 (b) is a development from them, and we can see the ideas here
being referred to again especially in 4, but also in the
parenthetic second line of 3 (a). Apart from these, the
ideas contained throughout this hymn are to be found
also throughout the gospel as we have seen it. Thus in
order to answer our question we really only have to examine this idea of the word as being with God and equal
to God, and of his having become flesh and dwelt
among us. If the content of 3 (a) and (b) are part of the
original hymn, as they seem to be, the connection between the word and his becoming flesh is made explicit,
and thus we are left simply with the task of looking at the
meaning and origin of the term 'word'.

Because of the close association of the term *logos*
('word') with Greek philosophical thought, together with
the high probability that the Johannine gospel developed
and emerged from the very Greek area of Ephesus,
people have looked for Greek patterns of thought in this
hymn to the word in the prologue, Platonist, stoic and
Hermetic. However, these similarities are all rather
tenuous and when one goes to the old testament and ex-
amines the parallels there it becomes obvious at once
that the connections involved are of a completely different order. Not only are there such connections, but most
of them tie in very closely with themes which are also
developed throughout the fourth gospel itself. We will do
no more here than present the parallels and indicate
some of the more important connections.

As a preliminary, one should notice that the prologue
contains a number of elements which are closely associated with prominent themes from the Pentateuch: eg
'in the beginning', 'creation', 'life', 'light' over against
'darkness', which relate to the creation narratives of
Gen 1–3; 'the glory of God', his 'dwelling (tenting)
amongst us', which are suggestive of the theophanies of
Sinai. All this would indicate without anything else that
there are close relations between the prologue's hymn
and the old testament. But there is a great deal else.

Two major and two minor old testament and later
judaic themes show marked similarity to this hymn to the
word. The two major ones are firstly the word of the
Lord in the prophets, which brings judgment and creates
life, and is sent out from God as a reality on its own to
work his will and bring men back to him (Is 55:11);
secondly personified wisdom. We have seen this coming
up again and again throughout the gospel. Wisdom
comes from the Lord and remains with him for ever

(Sir 1:1); is an effusion of the glory of the Almighty (Wis 7:25, 26). Wisdom was created from the beginning: 'Ages ago I was set up . . . before the beginning of the earth' (Prov 8:23); wisdom is divine, even if the Hebraic mind would not be able to identify it with God. There are good parallels for almost every detail of the hymn to the word in the wisdom literature.

The two minor themes are the law, and an Aramaic word originally meaning 'word' which, in the commentaries on scripture, had come to mean the 'presence' of God. The former is frequently thought of precisely as the word of God and in Sir 24:23ff and Bar 4:1 is identified with wisdom. With regard to the second we know that many of the Johannine references to scripture come from these very same commentaries.

The case for the Hebraic background and provenance of the ideas in the hymn is thus overwhelming. The advance made on this, ie the synthesis to be found in the hymn, is absolutely consonant with the theology which we have seen throughout the gospel. There remains one problem, and that is the choice of the word *logos* to describe all this, for the closest parallel is undoubtedly with wisdom. We have seen, however, that in three out of the four themes which we have looked at, the idea of word, in one form or another, is a dominant aspect. One can add to this the important way in which *logos* was being used to describe the propagation of Christ's presence amongst future believers (Jn 17:20; Mk 4:14, 15).

It is possible that the philosophical connotation of *logos* in the Greek thought of the day was also a slight influence on the choice of this word, but it would seem unlikely when one considers the fundamental dissimilarity between Johannine and hellenistic thought. One can speculate that we might be being offered here what

John sees as the true *logos*, the true essence of and power behind all life in contrast to the ineffectual Greek search for similar depth—but it would be little more than speculation.

If this solution to the problem of the meaning and provenance of 'word' in the prologue can be taken for granted, there remain very few obscurities. It becomes abundantly clear, especially now that we are looking at it after we have seen the rest of the gospel, that it is in effect a conclusion to the gospel. It looks as if it grew up as a hymn within the Johannine community, for as we can now see it is Johannine through and through. It would then seem to have acquired a theological commentary, and together with this or slightly later to have been grafted into the beginning of the gospel as its introduction. As an expression of the themes which run backward and forward throughout the gospel we can now see how utterly non-abstract it is; it is an extreme condensation of the Johannine depiction of reality—the reality which is life-giving through God's presence in Christ.

For the most part the commentary attached to the hymn is developed in terms which we have come across throughout. In one or two places, however, the terminology, if not the idea, is new, and at times the language, especially in English translation, is puzzling. 1:12, forming the antithesis of 1:11, contains one of the primary messages of the gospel, but the author is very particular to stress that becoming the children of God is something which itself comes from God (1:13). This verse acts as a bridge and leads into the idea of the word itself becoming flesh, ie human, and taking up his abode (dwelling = 'tenting') there. God comes fully amongst men, but man's presence to him is through God's power.

not through man's—this is the point, and it is an 'emphatic condensation' of what occurs throughout the gospel. 'Full of grace and truth' (1:14) qualifies this presence. Here is a phrase which, almost certainly, refers to the 'steadfast love and truth' of God which is spoken of throughout the old testament. This is the covenant love between God and man; in this case the love of the new covenant. (The Greek used by John is characteristically a slight variant of the normal Septuagint rendering of the term.)

The concluding verses (1:16–18) contain a highly condensed and carefully articulated message. We, who believe in the incarnate word, receive from his fullness. This is 'grace upon grace', or in other words this is divine gift being added to an earlier gift. This latter is immediately identified: the law of Moses (1:17a). This was the first expression of covenant love; but to this has been added a further, a new, covenant love: the 'grace and truth' which comes from Jesus (1:17b). It might seem at first sight that these two are being contrasted here and the former rejected in favour of the latter; but this is only apparent in the translation, which misses the nuances. John's attitude to the law is quite clear; it is the word of God which is fulfilled personally in Jesus—fulfilled not rejected. The nature of this fulfilment is expressed in the final lines (1:18): Moses who gave the law never saw God; but Jesus, being the Son of God, of his very nature sees God because his rightful place is in the bosom of the Father, and from this position he communicates the life and the vision of the Father to us. The prologue thus ends by returning on itself: the Son in the bosom of the Father is paralleled with the word who was with God from the beginning. Note how the language of the 'commentary' is closer to that of the gospel than is the lan-

guage of the hymn—but they fit together without difficulty, and they fit in equally with the whole gospel.

Manifestly the prologue has a life of independent development within the same school as the gospel: and
equally its relationship to the latter is one of dependence,
for its meaning is not clear without this latter. Seen in
terms of the gospel the prologue is a high condensation
of the former's doctrine, but not an abstraction from it.
As an introductory 'conclusion' to the gospel the prologue, for all its incandescence, shares the gospel's
realism.

*1. How effective a summary of the gospel is the prologue?
Has the gospel gained or lost by having this conclusion placed at
its beginning?*

*2. Is the 'word' the fulfilment of the 'law'? In what way does
this bear upon whether christianity is or is not truly speaking a
religion?*

Conclusion

If the prologue is itself a conclusion what else can be
said? After such incandescence, what would not be flat?
A summary of the gospel's themes would be nothing but
misleading; their life is intrinsic to the way they are
interwoven and developed and organically related to
each other, forming a living whole. To abstract them
would be to kill them and turn them into unrealities.

One thing, however, can be done, and needs to be
done. After such a richness as that which we have seen,
have explored and almost felt with our senses, we are in
danger of being overwhelmed. In order to regain perspectives a small number of the gospel's characteristics
will be pointed to.

The most prominent, and possibly the most important, of these is the gospel's realism. It has often been thought of as the 'spiritual' gospel. That it can fairly claim this I think we can agree; but its spirituality lies in and depends upon a radical and living contact with reality. That the contact with reality is living is the important point. Facts tend to be dead ciphers; reality is related to facts as the living is to the dead, and John's gospel takes up the 'facts', never in effect allowing them to be merely this, and through its dramatic movement and poetic expression turns them into life. It is not history in any ordinary sense of the term; it is not theology in the sense in which this has often come to be understood. And yet it is profoundly about God; and also, if it is not history, it is nevertheless historical—again and again we have seen how it has a closer relationship to its origination than was ever once suspected. And the poetry and the drama with which it presents its message maintain that link, and yet at the same time project its significance forward into the world, through it, and beyond it. The spirituality and the realism of the gospel reflect (both metaphorically and literally) the presence of God to man in the incarnation—the word made flesh and dwelling among us.

The movement and the reality are dependent, in their expression, upon the dialectical tension which the drama holds and unfolds to us. We have seen how Christ brings judgment, how he confronts the world, forcing it to take sides for or against him, how he divides it. The flow and action of the gospel depend upon this, they advance with its power, and it can as a result bring that same confrontation into the world around us today. It is not a message of comfort but of confrontation.

But at the same time it is a message of 'comfort', for

the paraclete is the comforter, and the gospels bring the paraclete. The 'comfort' is the strength that we, who believe in Christ, have by being one with each other and thus one with him, for the life of the paraclete is the life which Jesus shares with his Father and which is now shared by those who believe in his name. The idea of community, of fellowship between man and man in order to make Christ's presence a reality is not spelled out in the fourth gospel, but it is implicit throughout it, implicit in the drama, partially explicit in the discourses, almost totally explicit in Christ's prayer. That it is the gospel of an individualist spirituality is easy to refute, because that idea is based on a concept of spirituality nowhere to be found in the gospel.

But the comfort of community is not something which is cosy; the dialectic tension is there throughout. Nor is community an end in itself. In sharing Christ's life we see the Father; in seeing the Father in Christ we fall down and worship him, but he lifts us up, calling us no longer servants but friends. The reality of the gospel is something which has to be lived out in all its dimensions.

1 John

Bernard Robinson

Introduction

We shall refer to the author of this epistle, according to convention, as 'John'. This is not to be taken as indicating a conviction that the epistle had the same author as the fourth gospel (though John A. T. Robinson, *inter alios*, has argued strongly and plausibly for this), still less that the author can, after such an interval of time, be definitely identified with John, son of Zebedee, the beloved disciple. What is clear, and what alone matters in this connection, is that the epistle bears strong linguistic and theological affinities to that gospel: both surely spring from the same milieu, and both are at least products of what can be called the school of the beloved disciple; even if he did not personally write either of them—a very plausible hypothesis—they both see events through his eyes and in the perspective of his thought and preaching. Despite some slight differences in outlook between them (indicated by C. H. Dodd, and perhaps exaggerated by him), the same spirit pervades them both, a spirit quite different from, say, that of Paul.

1 John is called a 'catholic' or 'general' letter, in the sense that it is not addressed to any one individual or church. Yet the author presumably had some particular group in the church in mind as he wrote, and it is important to try to discover who they were, as will be appreciated later.

Whereas the purpose of the fourth gospel was 'that you
may believe . . .' (Jn 20:31), which perhaps indicates that
the gospel was written to convert the unbelieving or the
hesitant to Christ, the author of the epistle says 'I write
this to you who believe in the name of the Son of God,
that you may know that you have eternal life' (5:13) and
'I write to you, not because you do not know the truth,
but because you know it' (2:21), thereby indicating that
the purpose of his letter is to reassure believers, confirm
them in the faith, and put them on their guard against
false teaching (a number of tests of orthodoxy are given
in the epistle, usually beginning 'By this we know . . .').

Were the recipients of the epistle Jewish or gentile, and
what were the heretical tendencies of which they must
beware? J. A. T. Robinson has shown very good grounds
for concluding that John was writing to Jewish christians,
not gentiles as is generally supposed. A few of his points
may be repeated here. In the first place, the categories of
thought are Jewish—the author uses *the Christ* as a title
(not *the Lord*, which was the title for Jesus among the
gentiles, who had come to treat *Christ* as a proper name),
and he uses terms like *false prophecy* (4:1), and *antichrist*
(2:18; 4:3), which would fall more meaningfully on
Jewish than on gentile ears. Again, the moral viewpoint
is Jewish, as evidenced by such expressions as 'everyone
who commits sin is guilty of lawlessness; sin is lawlessness' (3:4): this is very much a Jewish viewpoint—the
sinner, John is saying, is not even keeping the law. The
argument would not have been very telling to a gentile,
especially an antinomian gentile (for the recipients of the
epistle are commonly supposed to have been antinomian
gentiles): writing to such people John would surely have
reversed this saying and have written 'all lawlessness
is sin'. For me, the argument for a Jewish audience is

clinched by 2:22–3: 'This is the antichrist, he who denies
the Father and the Son. No one who denies the Son has
the Father. He who confesses the Son has the Father also.'
This exactly fits Jews, who claimed God for their Father
while not recognising the Son.

The heretics, the antichrists, against whom John had
to warn his 'little children', seem to have taught two things
chiefly: first, that Jesus is not the Christ (2:22; 4:3 etc);
and secondly, that sin either does not exist, or at least that
it is of no consequence (3:4 etc). From the emphasis
that John lays upon deeds and the necessity for a practical
form of love, it seems likely that the heretics thought
themselves absolved from the need actually to *do* anything. All this fits in very well with the sort of position
that a gnostic Jew of the first century might have taken
up (for instance, Cerinthus, who has traditionally, from
the time of St Irenaeus onwards, been thought of as the
main adversary of St John). Such a gnosticism was
dualistic, and attributed sin to the influence of matter:
the elect were saved by knowledge (*gnosis*) and did not
have to worry about actions, good or bad, for actions
belonged to the body, which was of no account. John, on
the contrary, insists on the importance of actions, and the
necessity of good deeds for salvation; there is no salvation for the sinner whose evil actions have not been
atoned for (1:7; 2:1; 4:10). The gnostic is wrong to
suppose that the evil deeds done in the body do not
matter, that 'sin' is just an inevitable physical part of our
natural make-up, engendered by the evil principle that
resides in matter: in fact sin is a disastrous reality which
needs to be removed—Christ came 'to *destroy* the works
of the devil' (3:8); he came not to save us despite our sins,
but to eradicate our sins, so that we shall no longer be
sinners but just: 'No one born of God commits sin; for

God's nature abides in him, and he cannot sin, because he is born of God' (3:9). So anxious is John to oppose the antinomianism of the gnostic position, and to set against it the orthodox position that God does not connive at sins but obliterates them, that at times he says things which have led some to suppose that he believed that post-baptismal sin was impossible, but texts like 2:1 ('My little children I am writing this to you so that you may not sin; but if anyone does sin, we have an advocate with the Father, Jesus Christ the righteous'; cf 5:16) show that John did not in fact believe in the impeccability of the believer, and if his words seem sometimes to imply that he did, that arises out of his anxiety to rebut the dangerous heresy that there is no conflict between sin and grace.

John's method of apologetic repays study. He was, we have seen reason to believe, writing against Jewish gnostics (perhaps lapsed Jewish christians—cf 'they went out from us, but they were not of us', 2:19), men who employed such slogans as 'We are born of God', 'We are in the light', 'We have no sin', 'We dwell in God', all of which they meant in the light of their basic tenet of 'the distinction between the realm of light and the realm of darkness which is the material world, and deification through supernatural knowledge (*gnosis*)' (Dodd). John takes up each of these slogans and makes it his own, but in an orthodox sense, meeting the heretics on their own ground (a good apologetic ploy). It is indeed through the knowledge of God that we are saved, but this knowledge is no ethereal thing on a separate plane from our ordinary living: the knowledge which justifies has in it more of what we mean when we speak of knowing a person than of the knowledge of a theorem. To know God is to live, abide in and with him in a community of personal relationship, and personal relationships are practical rather than ethereal things. Moreover, God has so disposed things that our 'knowledge' of him is achieved and lived out not in isolation but in a community setting, so that there is no loving God without loving the household of the faith. To sin, by rebelling against God's commands or by steeling our heart against our brother whom God has loved, is to snap the bond of community both with God and with our brother. The knowledge of God, then, is not the flight of the Alone to the Alone through some super-sensitivised sort of thought-process; it is grounded in the material world, which so far from being itself the realm of darkness is the only way of access to God: the God we worship has manifested himself to us through our senses ('That ... which we have heard, which we have seen with our eyes, which we have looked upon and touched with our hands', 1:1). Thus—to illustrate John's metamorphosis of gnostic slogans—the christian can indeed say with the gnostics 'the whole world is in the power of the evil one' (5:5), but he understands the expression quite differently from them: it is only when the world has not been brought within the ambit of God's spirit that it is ruled by Satan; when any part of the world is touched by God's love, it ceases to be 'the world', in the sense in which the new testament uses the phrase (ie the world as organised in opposition to God) and is taken up into the great sacramental activity of the fellowship of the sons of God.

It is generally accepted now that the gospel and epistles of John reveal, more than any other books of the new testament, some striking affinities with the writings of the Qumran sectaries. It is unlikely that the author of either the gospel or the epistles had any close personal knowledge of the 'monks of Qumran', but the ideas of the sect were perhaps fairly widespread in Jewry, and it is not impossible that John the Baptist was personally involved with the community at one time, and was perhaps the channel whereby members of the christian church came into contact with the categories of Qumran thought.

Reading the scrolls, one finds oneself again and again smiling as one happens upon phrases familiar to us from the Johannine literature—'to do the truth' (1 QS 1:5; 5:3; 8:2; cf Jn 3:21; 1 Jn 1:6), 'to walk in the truth' (1 QS 4:6, 15; cf 2 Jn 4; 3 Jn 3), 'witness of the truth' (1 QS 8:6; cf Jn 5:33; 18:37). What strikes one most of all in the scrolls is the idea of the spirit of truth and the spirit of error: eg 'He created man to rule over the earth, designed two spirits for him in which to walk until the time fixed for his visitation, namely the spirits of truth and deceit. From a spring of light emanate the generations of truth, and from a well of darkness emerge the genera- tions of deceit' (1 QS 3:17 ff; tr P. Wernberg-Møller). The actual expressions 'spirit of truth' and 'spirit of error' are found only in 1 Jn 4:6, but the influence of the idea of the two spirits—truth and error, light and darkness—per- vades the entirety of the epistle. Of course, the idea of the two ways goes right back to Deuteronomy (30:15–20: 'See I have set before you this day life and good, death and evil ... therefore choose life, that you and your descendants may live'), but the particular forms in which this ancient Jewish idea was worked out at Qumran and in 1 John are too close for them to be totally inde- pendent developments from one old testament source. The two following examples may help to illustrate this closeness of thought:

1. Both the scrolls and 1 John contain the idea that the man who walks in the way of light cannot *stumble*: cf 'all

the spirits which are allotted to (the angel of darkness) strive to make the sons of light stumble, but Israel's God and his true angel help all the sons of light' (1 Qs 3:24) with 'He who loves his brother abides in the light, and there is no cause for stumbling' (1 Jn 2:10).

2. Both the sectaries and John are concerned to emphasise the disruptive nature of sin. Sin is not just an offence against God, a black mark in the heavenly account book, so to say; it breaks up the bond of community between God and men and between man and man. The sinner, say the scrolls, 'is not righteous when he walks in the stubbornness of his heart; in darkness he looks upon the way of light, and (with) perfect ones he cannot be reckoned. He cannot purify himself with atonement nor cleanse himself with waters of purification ... unclean, unclean he is, as long as he rejects the statutes of God, so that he cannot be instructed within the community of his counsel. For it is by the spirit of God's true counsel that the ways of man, all his sins, are atoned, so that he can behold the light of life. It is by the holy spirit of the community in his truth that he can be cleansed from all his sins ... Then he will be accepted by an agreeable atonement before God, and it shall be unto him a covenant of everlasting community' (1 Qs 3). To John likewise the core of true religion is contained in the idea of community or fellowship (a word, this, incidentally, which has played a great part in the literature of the reformed tradition, but until recently the fullness of the meaning of the word, in all its literalness, has scarcely been appreciated in any of the christian churches—except perhaps the orthodox church?): 'That which we have seen and heard we proclaim also to you, so that you may have fellowship with us; and our fellowship is with the Father and with his Son, Jesus Christ' (1

Jn 1:3). This fellowship cannot be taken for granted, for to sin is, says christian as well as Qumran theology, to break it and to separate ourselves from the community which gives meaning to our lives: 'If we say that we have fellowship with him while we walk in darkness, we lie and do not live according to the truth' (1 Jn 1:6).

NOTE. This commentary was written before the publication of J. C. O'Neill's *The Puzzle of 1 John*, with its interesting theory that 1 John is a collection of traditional writings of a Jewish sectarian movement which were revised when most members of the sect went christian. A number of difficult texts in the epistle make good sense if we see them as originally embodying the pre-christian sentiments of a community akin to the Qumran settlement, which were later reinterpreted, sometimes by something of a *tour de force*, in a christian sense.—B.R.

1

Walking in the path of light
1 Jn 1:1–2:29

1 Jn 1:1–4

The letter begins with what is perhaps the quintessence of Johannine theology, the idea that Christ is, as we should say, the primordial sacrament. To John the incarnation involved no humiliation, no *kenosis* (there is no Johannine parallel to Phil 2), no concealment of divinity: God became man that he might reveal himself to men and be present to them in the way that human beings are present to one another, namely through their senses.

In the fourth gospel all the senses are resumed under the idea of seeing, which is given great prominence (eg 1:14, 29, 36, 39, 46, 50; 6:40; 12:21; 14:9, 19; 16:16; 17:24; 19:35), but these verses at the beginning of this letter emphasise the multiplicity of the senses with which the apostles came into contact with Christ. Unlike the apostolic generation, *we* are dependent on hearing only ('that which we have seen and heard we proclaim unto you', 1 Jn 1:3: the apostles had both seen and heard but their disciples could only hear): '*auditu solo tuto creditur*', as St Thomas was to write. Is not this, at bottom, what puts the apostolic church in such a superior position to all subsequent ages, and ultimately lies behind the idea of biblical inspiration? The scriptures are the ultimate in

christian theology because they are the expression of the
apostolic experience; it was God's will that we should
know him through the definitive experience of him which
the apostolic generation alone enjoyed. This experience
the church of the apostles has mediated to us in the
written word. The canon of scripture was closed at the
end of the apostolic age precisely because the age of the
plenary or apostolic experience of God-in-Christ had
ended—all those who had seen with their eyes, looked
upon and touched with their hands were now dead—
and the future task of the church was to transmit that
experience, not to add to it (see Rahner, *Inspiration in the
Bible*, in the *Quaestiones Disputatae* series).

*What part does the idea of community play in our theology?
What relevance has it to the liturgical movement? And to the
ecumenical movement?*

1 Jn 1:5–2:11

John begins his attack on the 'sinless' gnostics (see the
Introduction), showing that antinomianism undermines
the very basis of christianity. He propounds a practical
test of true religion—the imitation of Christ (2:6).

Like the men of Qumran John divides the human race
without remainder into saints and sinners, those who
walk in the path of light and those who walk in the path
of darkness. However, his division is not as clear-cut as
that of his antinomian adversaries. They held that once a
man, through *gnosis*, entered the path of light his future
was secure, and no action of his could affect his fate. Not
so, says John: if a man should, subsequently to his
baptism, commit sin, the true interpretation of the
situation is that he has slipped back and crossed into the

other path again—he no longer abides in God. We today will be inclined to ask whether John's framework for his theology, namely the motif of the two ways, is not too inflexible to give full expression to his ideas. Do not sins vary in gravity? Surely not all sins totally sunder the bond with the ecclesial community? John seems to admit the justification of objections to the over-neatness of his system when he writes, at the end of his letter, 'though all wrongdoing is sin, not all sin is deadly sin' (5:17).

We must beware of taking 2:2 ('he is the expiation for our sins') too crudely. Nothing could be less christian than the idea of a fuming deity being placated by the offer of a few pints of warm blood. Few christians today, one hopes, think of the sacrifice of Christ in quite such a crude way as that, but many do think of it in terms of a tariff of punishments: when a wrong is done, the 'scale of justice' (whatever that means—nothing at all, I suspect) must be redressed by a stipulated quantity of suffering; the broken fellowship of man with God can only be mended if someone 'pays the price'. This is quite un-biblical, as well as being philosophically absurd and morally monstrous (it makes God a congenital sadist). Such words as sacrifice, propitiation and expiation in the new testament are purely metaphorical. Christ 'takes away' the sin of the world not because he bears the suffering required by justice to obliterate them from the divine account book, but because his voluntary death is a revelation of love, and an invitation. Our sins are for-given through Christ in the sense that it is by coming into fellowship with him, the primordial sacrament, by sharing through baptism—and ultimately through death—the total self-surrender of Christ, that we are rescued from ourselves and begin to live the life of God.

1 Jn 2:13–14 constitutes something of a puzzle. Why the separate mention of 'children', 'fathers', and 'young men'? Why the change of tense from 'I write' (verse 12 and 13*a*) to 'I wrote' (verse 13*b* and verse 14. Some English translations cover up the difficulty by giving present tenses in both cases)? Did John mean 'I write *because* . . .' or 'I write *that* . . .' (the Greek *hoti* can mean either)? Perhaps these questions are unanswerable (for theories, see the commentaries). The thought does occur to one, however, that the passage is very, very rhetorical —almost poetic, in fact—and it does make great play of the idea of knowledge (*gnosis*); is it possible that John is parodying a gnostic hymn or ritual in order to emphasise that it is really the christians, not the gnostics, who know God?

1. We tend to see things nowadays less in black and white than the apostles did, and probably should tremble to say of ourselves that we 'walk in the light'. Is this perhaps partly because we are more guilt-ridden than the men of the apostolic age (though 3:20 shows that 'scruples' were known then too)? Do we perhaps need to revise our theology of guilt?

2. What is one to make of 'propitiation'?

1 Jn 2:15–17

John reminds us that there is a certain irreducible element of exclusiveness about christianity. We have passed from darkness to light, and there must be no backward glances towards the Egyptian fleshpots, no hankering for the ways of the 'world'. John is not, as might at first be thought, joining forces with the gnostics to condemn as evil the world of material things; he uses the expression 'the world' in the technical new testament sense, meaning 'the world as apart from God its creator, the world as self-sufficient, consequently running counter to its creator, and thus evil in its tendency' (Souter). Souter suggests that the word may have acquired its pejorative sense from such texts as Is 13:11, where 'the world' is used to indicate 'the sum of the fierce surrounding heathen nations, the powers of the heathen world, at once destructive and corruptive'.

How do we achieve a mean between retreating from the world and becoming so involved in it that we lose the sense of redemption from all that the world becomes apart from Christ?

1 Jn 2:18–29

It is not the gnostics who possess the true *gnosis*, but the christians, who have been anointed with the spirit of truth: 'You have been anointed by the Holy One, and you know everything'. In this knowledge they must 'abide', not seeking to improve upon it in the name of some desire for 'progress' through adoption of gnostic ideas (cf 2 Jn 9: 'Progressives who do not stand by the doctrine of the Christ are without God').

'Children, it is the last hour.' How seriously are we to take the idea of the second coming? Several of the earlier Pauline epistles evince a clear belief that the parousia was very near at hand, whereas in the later epistles it is seen as more distant. This is at least a warning to us not to take inspiration as referring to particular sentences in the new testament instead of to the whole corpus of books, which together express the apostolic experience. To suppose that every fragment of the new testament must be swallowed just as it stands, that the whole of God's truth is distilled drop by drop, sentence by sentence, would require us to acquiesce in Paul's misogyny as well as his contradictory statements about the parousia. If the new testament were, in fact, revelation doled out in a series of true propositions, the occasional nature of it would be difficult to understand; the reason, I suggest, that so much of it is so occasional is that it is through occasional writings that we can best see the apostolic church as she lived and moved, and can thus capture the feeling of her daily life and her all-important experience.

All the same, do we not tend today to underestimate the importance of the parousia?

'It is the last hour.' Is it?

2

Breaking with sin
1 Jn 3:1–24

The thought of this chapter presents no great difficulty.
John insists, against the gnostics, on the reality of sin
(3:4–10): grace and sin are contradictions ('he who does
right is righteous', 3:7). But it is not enough not to sin,
we must practise love (3:11 ff), a genuine love revealing
itself in action. The fact of doing acts of love is a practical
test of our religion, not just for others but for ourselves
too—in moments of scrupulosity it should reassure us:
'Love must be genuine and show itself in action. That is
how we may know that we belong to the realm of truth,
and convince ourselves in his sight that even if our conscience condemns us, God is greater than our conscience
and knows all' (3:19, 20).

*1. 'The reason the Son of God appeared was to destroy the
works of the devil'. What place has the devil in our theology?*

*2. 'By this we know that he abides in us, by the Spirit which
he has given us.' How does one recognise the presence of the Spirit—
by charismata such as miracles and inspired preaching, or by
internal experience? How in a divided christendom does the Spirit
reveal himself?*

3
Love and faith
1 Jn 4:1–5:12

1 Jn 4:1–21

The chapter begins with two practical tests of orthodoxy:

1. 'Every spirit which confesses Jesus as the Christ come in the flesh is of God.' This perhaps against the adoptionist view which Irenaeus attributes to Cerinthus: 'Jesus was not born of a virgin, but was the son of Joseph and Mary, a man like other men except that he surpassed them in righteousness, prudence and wisdom. After his baptism, there descended upon him, from the sovereign power which is above all things, the Christ in the form of a dove; thereafter he revealed the unknown Father and worked miracles; but at the end the Christ departed again from Jesus, and it was Jesus who suffered and rose again, whereas the Christ continued impassible, being a spirit.'

2. The second test of orthodoxy is willingness to accept the *magisterium* of the church. 'We are of God. Whoever knows God listens to us. By this we know the spirit of truth and the spirit of error.' In 4:4 John had said 'You are of God'; he repeats this now, but changing the pronoun to 'we', presumably because 'the teachers and not the whole body of Christians are meant' (Brooke). St John introduces here, says P. Bonsirven, 'the criterion of

the *catholica* which St Augustine invoked against the Donatists, a criterion that simple men can easily use: obedience to the *magisterium* shows whether a spirit is of God or not'.

Are practical tests of orthodoxy relevant today?

1 Jn 5:1–12

This section commences with a reaffirmation of the 'test' of love in action. In 5:6, John goes on to offer a criterion not of our own conduct or orthodoxy, but of the truth of Christ's claim: our belief in Christ is attested, says John, by the threefold witness of spirit, water, and blood. This text has been interpreted in various ways. An ingenious explanation is offered by W. Nauck, in terms of the ancient baptismal practice of Syria, where the anointing and gift of the spirit seem to have preceded baptism: thus the order was (1) spirit, (2) water (baptism), (3) blood (the eucharist). If this explanation is correct, John is appealing to our sacramental experience as an evidence of the truth of the christian revelation. Others explain the 'three witnesses' in historical terms, in reference to the baptism and crucifixion of Christ (although a secondary sacramental motif is not to be excluded): the fact that Jesus was baptised with water in Jordan, and shed blood on Calvary, shows that he was no phantom, and this is confirmed by the work of the spirit in the life of Christ and of the church. Perhaps the best way is to take all three witnesses as referring to the crucifixion: Jn 19:35 strongly emphasises that water and blood issued from the side of Christ—probably the early church made so much of this fact because they saw it in the light of a rabbinic tradition (Exodus R 122 *a*;

Targum Num 20:11) that when Moses struck the rock
both water and blood emerged (though the old testament
mentions water only): so the emergence of water and
blood from Christ proved him to be the real rock of God
(cf 1 Cor 10:4). As for the spirit, note that in John Jesus
did not 'give up' his spirit on dying but 'handed on the
spirit' (*paredōke*; Jn 19:30)—thus passing his spirit on to
his disciple as Elijah had done: in the Johannine view,
therefore, the spirit (the Holy Spirit) at the crucifixion is
an active agent, a symbolic witness to Jesus, together with
the water and the blood.

*John's apologetic seems to be such as would appeal to
christians only, not to unbelievers. Is there such a thing as
apologetics or, as some maintain, is all that we can do for the
unbeliever to preach the gospel to him?*

4

Conclusion
1 Jn 5:13–20

1 Jn 5:13–20

In this final section John reiterates some of the main points of his letter.

1. The true 'gnostics' are the christians, who 'know' God in a way inaccessible to the self-styled gnostics, ie at the level of personal relationship, so that they enjoy a *parrhesia* towards him (5:14)—that is, liberty of speech and the facility of access that friendship gives: the christian can speak to God without elaborate protocol, opening his heart to him, and confidently making requests of him—eg for grace for an erring brother (5:16).

2. The true-born christian does not sin. As we have seen, such statements in John are pre-theological, and require before they can be translated into cold theological formulation to be seen in the light of the whole letter. John is taking over the slogan of the gnostic, who meant by it that even if he sinned he was not a sinner, for he had been saved by '*gnosis*'; John's use of the phrase has quite a different meaning: sin and divine birth, regeneration, are sworn foes, and to be truly regenerate and remain in possession of the divine life a man has to stop sinning.

'Little children, keep yourselves from idols.' This may seem an odd ending for the letter, for no mention of the danger of idolatry has been made so far. But John is not, presumably, thinking of idols of wood and stone. The word *eidolon*, though in the new testament it always means an idol, has in classical usage another meaning too—the ghost of a dead person: thus the shades of the heroes whom Odysseus meets in Hades are termed *eidola*. John has just been stressing the utter realness of what the christian believes in—'we are in him who is *real*, in his son Jesus Christ. This is the *real* God and eternal life'—and when he goes on to warn his readers of *eidola* John is thinking of the insubstantial shadowy vapours that are gnosticism. You have known the truth, he says, do not return to the pursuit of will-o'-the-wisps. Thus the letter ends on the note on which it began—the belief, which is central to the christian faith, that God is no mere ethereal proposition, but a person who has encountered us in what a modern philosopher calls 'the familiar world of things, people, and events': 'That which was from the beginning, which we have heard, which we have seen with our eyes, which we have looked upon and touched with our hands . . . we proclaim also to you.'

What are the main eidola *which the apostle would wish to warn us of if he were writing today? Is perhaps a form of gnosticism one of them?*

James

Laurence Bright

Introduction

The importance of the epistle of James has often been misunderstood throughout christian history (Luther's rejection of it is only the most notorious example). Quite apart from the clash with Pauline theology over the relation between faith and works, which we shall have to look at in its place, the whole tone is quite different from that of the Pauline letters. There is, at first sight, very little doctrinal content. Jesus is hardly mentioned; there is no reference to his death and resurrection, so central for Paul in his struggle to make clear the christian situation over against judaism. Certainly James' letter is much more than the moral tract it has sometimes been made out to be. Its moral emphasis comes from a profound theology. But that is, precisely, a theology not a christology; it is because God is what he is that men must act in one way rather than another.

Because of this James has sometimes been thought of as Jewish rather than christian. This is certainly incorrect. The Jewish background is obvious enough, especially in the many parallels with the wisdom literature of the old testament, such as Proverbs, Wisdom, and Sirach; there is also borrowing from a second century BC work called the *Testaments of the Twelve Patriarchs*. But it is equally clear that James is familiar with the teaching of Jesus, especially as it was being developed in the

227

tradition that issued as the gospel of Matthew. We are particularly reminded of the collection of sayings that Matthew put out as the sermon on the mount, and of the attack on scribes and pharisees also characteristic of that gospel. James scarcely ever quotes directly, either from OT scripture or the teachings of Jesus, but he makes it clear that he is as familiar with the one as with the other.

Altogether, then, the letter can be said to represent an authentic early christian tradition which bears a close relationship to the communities spoken of in the earlier parts of Acts. Quite likely it was written in Palestine, and for christians who were Jews rather than gentiles in origin. While there are parallels with the late Pauline letters, especially Colossians, James stands on the whole for a very different approach, a theology that has often been overshadowed by the richness of Pauline thought, but which has come more into its own in recent times. As late capitalist society shows its inherent violence more openly, we find the straightforward concern for social justice expressed by James more appealing than the subtle compromises with pagan authority which mar the Pauline letters.

The evidence, then, points to a comparatively early date for the letter, say around 60 AD (this means that the close literary relationship with 1 Peter need not be considered here, since James is the earlier). What of the author? This is a comparatively minor matter, because the very general character of the writing shows it to be much less a 'letter' in our modern sense than a sermon or tract, reflecting the teaching common in the Palestinian church some twenty to thirty years after the death of Jesus. There is no good reason to deny the traditional authorship of James, 'brother of the Lord', who occurs frequently in Acts and Paul (Ac 12:17 etc, Gal 1:19 etc).

The Greek is said to be too good, and the mastery of the essentially hellenistic 'diatribe' form, consisting of questions and answers in an imaginary dialogue—eg 'Is any one among you suffering? Let him pray' (5:13). But there is no real way of telling whether or not this lay within the competence of the first leader of the Jerusalem church. He could well have produced the work before he was killed in 62 AD (Josephus *Ant* xx, 9.1). On the other hand 'James' was a common enough name, and the identification was made only a century or so later. What does it matter?

Book list

The standard commentaries, such as Peake, are worth looking at, but apart from them there is nothing very exciting.

James, Jude and 2 Peter, ed E. M. Sidebottom, *The Century Bible* (London 1967), is good for a sound exegesis but too technical for popular consumption.

The Epistle of James, E. C. Blackman, *The Torch Bible Commentaries* (London 1957), is easy to read but pietistic and long-winded.

1

God and man
Js 1:1–18

Js 1:1–8. The purpose of temptations

One can see from the first line that this is very far from being a letter in the Pauline sense. There is no greeting to a particular church, or group of friends. It is unlikely that James is a letter at all in Paul's sense, but rather a tract given letter-form artificially, as commonly happened in the ancient world.

Even as a tract it seems somewhat disjointed, compared with the developed argument of, say, Romans. James appears to skip from topic to topic in a disconcerting way. There is, nonetheless, a real and important argument here. James is writing about christian behaviour, in moral terms, but the standpoint from which he does so is the nature of God's goodness. This is unusual in the Jewish-christian tradition, where the standpoint is more often the action of God in the world. This, in fact, is where James himself begins, but soon moves away from. In this, and the following section (1:9–18), the movement of thought in each case is from the trials christians undergo to God who, though not their cause, makes them a source of life.

James starts abruptly with the statement that christians should rejoice in their trials and difficulties. Quite probably these are the ordinary problems of everyday life—

there is no specific reference to persecution, which had in any case not yet become usual. He takes it for granted that this joy in trial is the christian attitude, and indeed, the idea is fairly common throughout the new testament— eg Mt 5:11–12.

The argument now moves very quickly. The endurance of these trials results in steadfastness, not the stoic virtue but much more the deep trust in God that Job showed in his troubles (cf Js 5:12, where Job is specifically mentioned). But how are we to acquire such power? Simply by asking God. Here James is close to the tradition of the synoptic gospels, which no doubt goes back to Jesus himself: a single-minded trust that what we ask God for will be given (cf Mk 11:24; Mt 7:7–11). There is no sign of Paul's more developed theology, in which Jesus, risen and with God, mediates the gift. The gift asked for is wisdom; once again not the Greek intellectual virtue but the practical wisdom that is the main theme of the later books of the old testament. It is a practical morality, ranging from the banality of some of the proverbs to the profound teachings of the prophets.

Js 1:9–18. The goodness of God

First the idea that trials are a joy to the christian is developed further (9–12), and this time it allows James to reach the heart of his argument, the character of God (13–18).

The blessing of poverty is a familiar theme in the later old testament writings, from the great picture of the servant who brings new life to himself and others because of his sufferings (Is 52:13–53:12) to the rather smug and self-satisfied account of the oppressed sitting in judgment on their persecutors in Wisdom (Wis 2:10–3:9). The

theme is developed in the new testament, especially by
Luke, who in a key passage has Jesus open his ministry
with the quotation from Isaiah about the ending of
oppression (Lk 4:18-19; cf Lk 1:52-53). James contrasts
the exaltation of the poor with the humiliation of the rich
in a common platitudinous way, but throws in the odd
and not very consistent idea that this humiliation can
be a source of blessing to the rich man, presumably if he
accepts his losses in a christian spirit.

At this point James pulls himself back to the main line
of thought: endurance of trials leads to God's gift of 'the
crown of life'. But, he asks, was God the cause of the
testing which he rewards in this way? A long old testament tradition would have given a positive answer. The
classic example is the testing of Abraham to sacrifice
Isaac, from the eighth-century Elohist strand of Genesis
(Gen 22:1-19) or, a century or so later, the Deuter-
onomist's account of Israel's tests in the desert (eg Deut
8:2). Later still, the idea grew that God could not be so
directly responsible for these temptations, and Satan was
introduced (Job 1:7). But this hardly solves the problem,
for it is God who has to take the ultimate responsibility.
In fact it is rare anywhere in scripture to find James'
unequivocal statement that men alone are responsible
for their sins. This is not to say that the bible does not
everywhere accept that men must take full responsibility
for what they do; but no incompatibility was felt to exist
between this and the attribution of events to God. The
Hebrew world-picture was very different from that of the
Greeks, for whom necessity ruled gods and men alike,
and whose shadow was later to fall on christian theology
to create the problems of
      'fixed fate, freewill, foreknowledge absolute
      And found no end in wandering mazes lost'.

James now reaches the positive side of his teaching (1:16–18). God is not only not responsible for evil, he is the source of all good, and this is because he himself is free from any evil. Here James is close to the Johannine tradition: 'God is light and in him is no darkness at all' (1 Jn 1:5). But to talk in this way of what God is, rather than of what he does, is again unusual in the bible as a whole. The old testament speaks of God's acts, his control of human history: his goodness is his goodness to Israel, not his goodness in itself. The new testament extends this to the particular history of Jesus Christ, and its universal significance. Of course the other viewpoint does appear, especially in the Wisdom books, and again it is taken up and becomes far more common in later theology, where it leads to problems of reconciling the various 'attributes' of God.

Finally (1:18) James relates this to the truth that God is creator. This, once more, is a doctrine that developed late in the old testament, first in second Isaiah (eg Is 45:7, where both good and evil are created by God), then in the Priestly writers (Gen 1:1–2:3) and in Wisdom (eg Wis 9:1f). In speaking of 'the word of truth' James seems to have these last two in mind. The world is not an emanation from God, as the Greeks thought: it is something he decided freely to bring into being, and his mere word was enough. In the 'first-fruits of his creatures' there seems to be an echo of Gen 1:26, where man is God's likeness and image (cf Js 3:9). In the simplicity of this basis for the moral teaching that follows there is something very profound. No doubt James would have accepted the later Pauline idea that man is recreated in the risen Christ as true image of God (Col 1:15, cf 1 Cor 15:20–22). But here it is the simple fact of being human that gives man his dignity under God.

1. Does it make sense to talk about rejoicing in one's trials? Ought we to seek them if we aren't lucky enough to have them anyway?

2. How on earth can a christian believe that God will give him what he asks for, even if the request is for so worthy an object as endurance under trial?

3. The idea that it is good to suffer oppression seems deeply reactionary, leading people to accept without question the status quo. *Do you agree?*

4. Theologians down the centuries have agonised over God's goodness and the world's evil, God's omnipotence and man's freedom. It doesn't seem to worry the authors of scripture. Who is correct?

2

Belief and action
Js 1:19–2:26

Js 1:19–27. Christian praxis

The decks are now cleared for James to develop his moral
teaching. All good comes from God; how do we receive
it? By our response to the word of God. 'Word' is used in
a wide sense. It is the creative word of 1:18; but it is also
the commandments (the 'ten words' in Hebrew) or
better still the whole 'law'. 'Law' is a very inadequate
translation for *torah*, which covers all God's gifts to men
in deeds and words, and shows itself as the practical
wisdom that enables men to act rightly. So (1:22) we
have to 'do' this word, act it out, not merely receive it
intellectually. This near-identification of hearing and
doing, characteristically Hebrew rather than Greek, is
akin to the marxist notion of 'praxis'. Only in action do
we begin to understand, to grasp the theory that guides us.

This guidance of the *torah*, the 'perfect law of liberty'
is contrasted by James with purely natural resources in
the metaphor of the mirror (1:23–24). This description
of christian life as guided by a new law is closest to
Matthew's gospel, where especially in Mt 5–7, the
'sermon on the mount', Jesus is presented as a new Moses.
The contrast with Paul, for whom 'law' is replaced by
'spirit' (eg 2 Cor 3) can be overdone: Paul talks about the
'law of Christ' (Gal 6:2) for example.

In 1:26–27 James repeats the point in a paradoxical statement reminiscent of Amos or Isaiah (Is 1:11–17). 'Religion' means worship or liturgy, so James is asserting that the true liturgy is to bring about justice and mercy in the world, a point less often made by modern liturgical experts. This is not in fact contradicted by the final remark about being 'unstained from the world' when one remembers how *kosmos* is used, as in the Johannine writings, and rather as Paul uses 'flesh', to mean the world of injustice, exploitation and greed set in opposition to God. It is overcome by fighting it from within, not by running away (cf Jn 17:15–18).

Js 2:1–13. Rich and poor

The style now changes; James gives us two connected narratives (1–13; 14–26) in imaginary dialogue, the form known as 'diatribe' in the classical world. 2:1–7, with which the first discourse begins, is a savage attack on those who hold power and use it to exploit others. James would hardly have suffered from christian hang-up over engaging in our contemporary class-struggle.

This concern for social justice as a principal theme of the letter is in marked contrast with Paul (eg Rom 13:1–7) and comes close to the teaching of the synoptic gospels (eg Mt 19:16–26; 23:1–36; Lk 16:19–31). Significantly the section begins with the letter's only explicit reference to Jesus, apart from the introductory 1:1. The faith we act out is faith in Jesus (RSV 'of' is misleading) who is identified with the glory of God as given to men (cf Ex 33:7f, Jn 1:14. 'The Lord' has been inserted in the translations). Such faith is incompatible with 'partiality', siding with the rich and powerful against the poor. The illustration James provides scarcely needs comment.

Though in our own churches we no longer segregate rich and poor, the different catchment areas effectively do it for us, and anyway the poor wash more nowadays.

A short theological comment follows (2:5) relating to 1:17. God chooses the instruments by which to achieve his purpose in the world regardless of their intrinsic merit (cf Deut 7:6–7). As Israel failed, the choice fell on a section within the nation, the exploited (cf Zeph 2:3 and the commentary on Js 1:9–12 earlier). 1 Cor 1:27f is a characteristically Pauline expression of the idea. In Js 2:7 it looks as if the rich with whom the contrast is being made are themselves christian, though unworthy of the name. There is no warrant for relating this special role of the poor in Israel with that of the proletariat in capitalist society, though this is sometimes done by enthusiastic christian marxists. Nothing is said here about revolutionary action, only about the gift of God, though the two are not actually exclusive of one another. The 'kingdom' to be inherited is probably, as often in the synoptic gospels, the totality of God's blessings, but the context does not make it clear how the word is being used.

James now insists on the unity of the moral law (2:8–13). The phrase 'royal law' seems to mean the highest law we can recognise, the *torah* of God. The rabbinic summary of that law was two-fold: 'love God, love your neighbour' (cf Mk 12:19–31) and it is significant that here, as elsewhere in the new testament, the two parts are condensed into one (cf Gal 5:14; Jn 13:24; 1 Jn 4:20). In Christ love of man is also love of God.

This theme of the unity of the law makes it plain that James is not thinking of obedience to a set of moral imperatives, but rather of a complete attitude to moral action in every field. With its roots in the old testament (eg Jer 31:31f) this integrity of human behaviour in response to God is related elsewhere in the new testament to the gift of the Spirit transforming us in Christ.

Js 2:14-26. Faith and works

The section that follows has probably spilled more ink than the rest of the letter together. In itself it is straightforward enough: its interest is partly because it is obviously written in reply to Pauline ideas ('justification by faith alone', 2:24, occurs nowhere else in the new testament outside Galatians and Romans), so we must ask if the opposition is real or apparent. It is also of interest because its theme was a crucial issue at the reformation.

To take the text itself first. In 2:15–16, James repeats his example of christian moral action (2:2–4) but now to contrast such 'works' of love, done in faith, with 'mere' faith. He says nothing of 'mere' works (as for instance, Mt 25:31–36 seems to do). It is often asserted, on the basis of 2:19, that he is using 'faith' in the modern sense of intellectual assent to propositions, since then the tension between him and Paul is resolved: words would be being used differently. But this is clearly not true. The text, especially as it follows on the previous section about the integrity of the law, shows 'faith' to mean a deep attitude of trust in God, just as in the synoptic gospels (eg Mt 9:22), which affects all that we do (cf Mt 7:16f).

Faith in this sense is inseparable from its expression in action, the two making up an undivided christian praxis as in John (eg 1 Jn 2:4). Thus for James there cannot really be a faith without works, as there would be if it meant 'intellectual assent'. The man in 2:14 only claims to possess it, and in 2:17 it is non-existent, dead. 2:18 is ironical. In 2:19 mere intellectual assent would hardly

cause the demons to shudder: James means they experience the reality of God just as the christian does, but
because they are unable to act on it, it destroys them.

James now turns to the example of Abraham, perhaps
because of Rom 4, though Paul uses it very differently.
The willingness to sacrifice Isaac is again used for illustrat-
ing faith, trust in God, in Heb 11:17f. The point is made
explicit once more; faith and action together (2:22) lead
to justification by God. Abraham is 'counted righteous'
and enters into the covenant friendship with God. Here
it is the modern exegete who is made to shudder, by this
lumping together of Genesis passages from very different
traditions, but James would not have worried. He follows it by the similar example of Rahab (cf Heb 11:31)
The use of 'justified by works' is as polemical as Paul's
'justified by faith', for 2:26 again repeats the inseparabil-
ity of the two.

It is in fact Paul's strikingly original expression that
needs some explanation. It must be admitted that James
has failed to grasp the subtlety of his opponent's thought.
Subtle men are a nuisance to have around the church, as
a long line of heroes from Athanasius to J. H. Newman
could witness. Though Paul tried to forestall criticism
(eg Rom 3:8) James has produced such a caricature of
him that it is doubtful if he knew the letters at first-hand.
Paul is just as clear as he is that 'faith is working through
love' (Gal 5:6) and can quote 'he will render to every
man according to his works' (Rom 2:6). No more than
James would he ever divorce faith from its consequence
in moral action (eg Col 3:5–17) though his emphasis is
far less socio-political in choosing what that action should
be.

The difference therefore does not lie in the use of the
word 'faith', though Paul's idea, including as it does the

dimension of our relation to Christ, is more complex. It lies rather in 'works'. Rom 3–7 indicates that the Pauline attack is against the works of the Jewish law, rather than the works of christian love. He is combating the pharisaic position that had almost separated the law, in its elaborate detail, from God its giver. The four chapters are in effect an extended commentary on the parable of the pharisée and the publican (Lk 18:10–14). In the course of it, to be sure, Paul develops a profound theology of which there could be no trace in the parable. For in his insistence that justification and grace are beyond human power to acquire, being the gift of God, Paul is led to work out the foundation of this truth in an elaborate theology of the role of Christ, which moves far beyond the simple christianity of James, based on the words rather than the person of Jesus. Yet James makes the same point in his own way: 'every good gift is from above'.

But while it is one thing to agree that we are justified, made righteous, capable of acting morally well, through the gift of God alone, it is quite another to question what effect in that case moral acts have to modify our relationship with God. By the end of the middle ages popular catholicism had in practice often returned to the pharisaic belief that salvation could be wrested from God by ritual activities with little moral content, even when not corrupted by racketeers. Against all this Luther rightly made his protest, returning to the Pauline theology of the complete freedom of God's action to save us, independent of anything we do. The trouble is that such an argument pushed to its logical conclusion can make the individual relationship between a man and God the one thing necessary, without need for the church as the body of brothers in Christ, the sacraments as effectively showing forth that relationship, and so on. Eventually the link between grace and moral action is itself in doubt; if our actions not only do nothing to deepen our life with God, but we have to think of them all as worthless, it seems to matter less what we do. With Calvin we come closer to such a situation; good works are merely the proof and re-assurance of salvation. But then they are pursued by the elect with an individual fervour that relates little to those in less fortunate positions and thus unable to prove their credentials before God. Protestantism declined very differently from its predecessor, and showed its worst face in the smug and brutal spirituality of the nineteenth-century capitalist. No wonder that the writings of James became little thought of by comparison with his cleverer but perhaps less sensitive opponent.

1. Would you agree that to offend against one part of the moral law is to break all of it? A little sex on the side surely doesn't turn one into an exploiter?

2. Do you think christians today normally speak of 'faith' in the sense that James and Paul do? Would it be better if they did?

3. Do you think the controversy about faith and works is of practical importance? How far did it change the face of history?

3

Doers of the word
Js 3:1–5:20

Js 3:1–18. Teachers and their words

We can take the last three chapters much more rapidly.
There is a good deal of moral exhortation, exemplifying
the principle of the earlier sections, that being made in the
likeness of God who is all goodness, we must live this out
through the works we do. The trouble is that James, being
very general, lacks for us the interest of Paul, relating to
specific situations that have blown up in the churches
he founded. Moreover his generalities become somewhat remote against the totally different social-political
context of today. He rambles, he is at times banal, but
nonetheless he has good things to say on occasion and
he is at least blessedly short.

The first section relates, not too closely, to what is required of a teacher in the early Jewish-christian community. As one knows from Paul (eg 1 Cor 12:8f) the
teacher was highly regarded, and his responsibilities
were correspondingly great. When he failed, it was dis-
graceful. Nevertheless the attack on loose talk that follows
(3:2–12) strikes us as unnecessarily harsh. The central
point is made at 3:11; since God is pure goodness,
nothing but good can come from him (cf 1:17). We
should be the same (cf 1:18) yet our evil speech shows the
opposite. Speech, it is true, is so centrally a human

characteristic that a culture can be judged on its words: our own shouts violently at us through press, television, the advertising hoardings.

The following short section (3:13–18) takes up the theme of wisdom as required in a christian teacher (cf 1:5 and comment). James is thinking, especially at 3:17, of the well-known passage Wis 7:22–30 in praise of wisdom, centring, as does his own thought, on wisdom as the created reflection of God's light, offered to those he chooses.

Js 4:1–17. Further moral remarks

It is not easy to discover quite what James is on about in 4:1–12. 'Fighting among you' in 4:1 must refer to christians, yet it is hard to believe that things had reached a point where words like 'kill' could literally be applicable. But as in 1 Cor 1:10f, any division among those who claimed to love one another was a shocking thing, calling forth strong condemnation and the demand for repentance.

There follows a section on single-minded prayer to God, as in 1:5–7. The 'scriptural' quotation in 4:5 bothers the commentators, who can't track it down: maybe James was just bad at verifying his references. The ideas are familiar (they are found again in 1 Peter) and may well be drawn from well-known catechetical instructions in the early church. The last saying about humility and exaltation is familiar from the gospels (eg Mt 23:12, Lk 14:11 etc).

James now comes back again (4:11–12) to the harmfulness of loose speech, this time as offending against the 'royal law' of love (2:8). The evil-doer, instead of standing under the gospel law, sets himself up as its judge.

The need for humility is stressed once more in 4:13–17, which reads a bit like advice to christian executives; the contrast with Mt 6:34, 'do not be anxious about tomorrow', is piquant.

Js 5:1–20. The misery of riches: prayer

James at last gets back to his incisive self, echoing the remarks of chapter 1 with an all-out no-holds-barred attack on the rich (5:1–6). It is very much in the early prophetic tradition (eg Am 8:4–6). There is a close resemblance to some of the synoptic collections of the 'sayings of Jesus' (cf Mt 6:19–21; Lk 6:24–26). The contrast between the present life of the exploiter and his fate when God judges the world is in the manner of the parables (eg Lk 12:16–21). Nevertheless James does not question the economic structures themselves, only the injustices that some within them went in for, and his putting the solution off to the last judgment is still the people's opiate. There are overtones of Isaiah's servant in the righteous man (5:6) who does not offer resistance to his oppressors, and possibly of Jesus himself.

Js 5:7–11 continues the theme of patience instead of rebellion, which was no doubt the only thing that could be said to the poor and insignificant community of those days: the problems arise when such attitudes are treated as universally praiseworthy. The term *parousia*, translated 'the coming of the Lord', is a specifically christian one; the reference must be to the coming of Jesus, rather than of God (cf Mt 24:3, 1 Thes 4:15 etc) even though it is God who is being spoken of in 5:9–10. But James chooses old testament heroes, rather than Jesus, for his examples of patience in suffering (cf Heb 11), which echo and balance the opening section of the letter (Js 1:3–5).

Js 5:12, reminiscent of Mt 5:33–37, is unconnected with anything before or after.

The final section (5:13–18) in fact fits well after 5:11, for in it James follows the theme of steadfastness under trial by that of prayer, just as at the beginning (1:5–7). The trial now is sickness, and the prayer is accompanied by medical treatment. The Jews normally used oil to anoint the sick (cf Mk 6:13, Lk 10:34) but James makes it clear that the real cause of the cure is the prayer. The 'elders' are the leaders of the church (the term comes from the Jewish synagogue) who represent the whole community. We would probably place more reliance on the oil. It is particularly difficult for us to accept the link between sickness and sin, or sin and demonic power, but it is impossible to exorcise it from the new testament. Jesus himself is constantly described as healing because of his power to forgive sin, connected with his power over the demons (eg Mk 2:3–11; 20–27). Though the church later developed a sacrament from this practice, it can hardly be described as popular, and when we decide to ask for it we merely call the parish priest as quietly as we can, rather than make an affair of it with the prescribed elders.

The confession of sin (5:16) is related to the previous passage, since it is connected with the illness in some way, and is made to the elders. James once more turns to the old testament for an example of success in prayer, but it is somewhat unfortunate that in 1 Kg 17:1 nothing is said about Elijah having gone in for it before working his miracle.

Though there is no particular reason for finishing the letter at this point, James seems to have felt that enough was enough, and ends as abruptly as he began. Still the brief glimpse of the christian community loving and forgiving is a suitable conclusion to this account of christian praxis.

1. Would your own choice be for 'loose speech' (even in a wide sense) as the most significant evil of our own day?

2. Are you embarrassed by James' forthright attack on rich people (none of that stuff about separating the sinner from the sin) or would you like to see more of it?

3. Do you think it would be a good idea to ring up the parish elders for shared prayer whenever someone in the family (someone else, perhaps) felt ill?